Profit from Science

Profit from Science

Solving Business Problems Using Data, Math, and the Scientific Process

George Danner

First published in 2015 by
PALGRAVE MACMILLAN®
in the United States—a division of St. Martin's Press LLC,
175 Fifth Avenue, New York, NY 10010.

Where this book is distributed in the UK, Europe and the rest of the world,
this is by Palgrave Macmillan, a division of Macmillan Publishers Limited,
registered in England, company number 785998, of Houndmills,
Basingstoke, Hampshire RG21 6XS.

Palgrave Macmillan is the global academic imprint of the above companies
and has companies and representatives throughout the world.

Palgrave® and Macmillan® are registered trademarks in the United States,
the United Kingdom, Europe and other countries.

ISBN: 978–1–137–47484–1

Library of Congress Cataloging-in-Publication Data

Danner, George E.
    Profit from science : solving business problems using data, math, and the
scientific process / George Danner.
        pages cm
    Includes bibliographical references and index.
        ISBN 978–1–137–47484–1—ISBN 1–137–47484–X
        1. Problem solving. 2. Strategic planning. 3. Science—Methodology. I. Title.

HD30.29.D36 2015
658.4′03—dc23   2015009664

A catalogue record of the book is available from the British Library.

Design by Newgen Knowledge Works (P) Ltd., Chennai, India.

First edition: September 2015

10 9 8 7 6 5 4 3 2 1

Printed in the United States of America.

To my amazing family.
Dream big. Travel far.

Contents

Illustrations

Figures

Tables

Acknowledgments

A dream team of people compiled this book, some of whom had no idea they were doing so. Because I have drawn largely from my experiences, those who influenced my thinking and bestowed fragments of their own knowledge to me deserve to be recognized for their contribution to this work.

Jim Thomas was my first "real" boss at the engineering firm CRSS. Jim taught me the value of relationships with clients, the unspoken rules of engagement to get things done in a forest of agendas and egos.

MIT professor John Sterman taught me to think in systems. He handed me a pair of glasses, I put them on, and the world to me was never the same. No other teacher in my life had the kind of impact he did.

Sam Israelit, former partner, Arthur Andersen Business Consulting, was my first encounter with an uber problem solver. His mastery of complex and noise-filled challenges formed the template that underlies this book.

Tom Elsenbrook, former partner, Arthur Andersen Business Consulting, is the greatest team builder this world has ever seen. He built a team—I was part of that—and his imprint showed me how highly successful problem-solving teams really work, at the high-water mark of professionalism and integrity.

Stephen Wolfram, CEO of Wolfram Research, is the most brilliant individual I have ever met. His grasp of an astonishing range of scientific disciplines coupled with his keen business acumen is a thrill to see up close. Stephen's vision allowed me to connect the dots between science and business, a link that now defines my professional life.

To my colleagues at Business Laboratory, Alan Savoy, Tripp Lybrand, and Miles Hill: Alan, as the world best human debugger, you've pulled me out of more scrapes than I can count, for which I am forever grateful. Tripp, thank you for letting me see that writing a book was even possible, and for expertly caring for clients while I did so. Miles, after working with you, I believe that every company should have an ex-US Marine who also happens to be a physicist.

David Peregrine-Jones, Managing Director, Torus Business Web, Ltd, London, my business partner in the United Kingdom, gave me the intellectual grounding for the book and helped shape its direction based on a few hastily assembled notes.

Gerald Ashley of St. Mawgan & Co. Ltd, London, took a random conversation and used that to convince me to write a book and seek a publisher.

My editor, Laurie Harting, at Palgrave Macmillan supported me as a relatively new author with a level of patience that deserves some sort of medal, perhaps even a tiara.

I have been blessed with an amazing woman, my wife, Kathy—my friend, my cheerleader, my rock. Thank you for understanding my irrational passion for rational thought.

Introduction

This book is about solving business problems using data, math, and methodical processes.

It evolved from my circuitous career path as an engineer, a programmer, a business consultant, and later as a founder of two business simulation companies.

Late in life, I came to realize that everything that I did all day every day was about solving problems. In fact, that is what everyone (to some extent) in every organization is doing all day every day. Think about that "to-do" list sitting on your desk or in your computer—my guess is that all but the most trivial tasks relate in some way to a larger "problem" you are chipping away at daily. Problems are the molecules of corporate life.

When I finally did come to the realization that most all activity is problem solving, I started to look around for examples of the best problem solvers in history whose knowledge could be easily packaged and imported into the domain of corporate operations. The motivation was clear—companies that solve problems better will be better companies. My current company, Business Laboratory, was founded to work with firms on this very subject.

At last I found the world's best problem solvers, bar none: scientists.

For two dozen centuries, we have had the scientific method, so fundamental to the understanding of classical sciences that we teach it universally very early in the formal education system. Yet we present it as just that—a means of accessing science. When it comes to the *meta* science of solving problems no matter where they lie, we seem to reinforce this idea that knowledge is all about generating a mental book of rules gained through experience. Want to solve a problem? "Go ask Sue down the hall—she's been doing that for 25 years and knows the answer." I see it over and over again in my work with companies and the people inside them (and the consultants who work with them).

Science, however, cherishes (1) hypothesis development, (2) the presence of evidence through experimentation, (3) objective reasoning, and (4) transparency of investigation. These bedrock principles are the reason science has been so successful at tackling the world's most difficult questions for over two millennia.

Modern capitalism by comparison has been around for a handful of centuries. The results have been impressive. Where free markets have flourished and the open exchange of ideas thrives we have seen extraordinary products and technologies emerge. Yet my own observations of lots of organizations show that there is a surprising lack of discipline, systematization, and objectivity when it comes to doing analysis as a means to solve some problem, be it in the supply chain, in optimizing processes, reducing costs, making smart decisions under uncertainty, or crafting long-range strategies in the midst of market chaos. Mimicking the best aspects of science is one way to inject sound principles into our everyday corporate problem solving. The last decade and a half of my career has been one long search for the best possible integration of scientific thinking into business problems. What I discovered along the way became the genesis for this book.

As we sit here today, there is keen interest in analytics, data science, and decision analysis—a few of the fundamental building blocks of migrating scientific methods into the business domain. This book can show how to make these broad disciplines work in practical ways on real-world problems, no matter the industry or context.

This answers the "why" part of the book, so now let me talk about the "who."

In our line of work we see lots of struggles. Hard-working and smart people show up everyday to get the job done right. Inevitably in analytics we see someone doing it "the hard way"—fumbling over vast and poorly structured spreadsheets to tell a complex story about some facet of the company's operations. Most of the time their analysis is dead right, but their effort to advocate for a change that will improve the company falls flat for the lack of solid methods, data-driven evidence, processes, mechanisms, and techniques. This book is dedicated to them—a silent fist bump to the lonely ones who have struggled to apply analytics and data to express an important issue.

Baskets of books on analytics come across my desk every month. Many have great writers and insightful thinking among their pages. Precious few are prescriptive in nature—unable to provide the reader with a practical, systematic means of implementing methods they suggest. Most can agree and even get excited by the notion of scientific principles applied to business problems. But there has to be action fueled by that excitement. This is the gap that I would like to close with this book.

You already solve problems every day. By following the principles outlined here, you will learn how to become a *better* problem solver. You will learn the ever-important *process* of problem solving, the analytical methods and their respective strengths, how to work with data, crafting compelling visualizations of the systems under study, and the software tools to make it all happen.

You will also discover that problem solving isn't all about...solving any given problem. It also concerns *how* you go about problem solution, the formulation of teams of people to do the work, and carefully absorbing future trends in the field.

The book underwent several design stages similar to the design of any engineered product. A portion of the design requirements related to the presentation of the concepts, and then a deliberate and carefully crafted reinforcement of the concepts through practical application guidance. There are **sidebars** when a specific point must be raised for emphasis. **Case studies** from our own work show how the principles are overlaid onto real business problems. **How-to** sections offer clear instructions on all of the mini-skills you will need to create your own analytic solutions.

And finally **FAQs** are my own "simulation" of the questions that I am guessing you will have along the way.

The companion website, http://www.business—laboratory.com/profit fromscience, provides the reader with an ongoing, ever updating resource to follow as the science of business analytics inevitably changes. Consider bookmarking that page and making a habit of visiting periodically.

If I have done my job correctly, you will finish this book having a keen grasp of the theory, the thinking, and the implementation skills to create a scientific renaissance inside your company. Again, better problem solving = better company.

You and I are partners now—we are going to be engaged in an important conversation together across these pages. And after the reading, the real work starts, and along with it the frustration, the pain, the joy, the doubts, and the victories, small and large.

Let's get started.

CHAPTER 1

Hello World

B usiness problems are everywhere, and they don't go away easily. Solve one, and ten more come across the desk. It seems that in the business of business, whether you are in a private corporation, a government agency, or a nonprofit organization, the picture in front of you is still the same: things are more complicated than they used to be. That means that we are all asked to solve problems at a faster rate than before, often with precious little data and dated tools. The stakes are higher. The signal-to-noise ratio is lower. There are fewer brains and bodies to help.

Any of these sound familiar?

How many trucks are needed to ship our products in the new territory?
Process X in our organization is clearly broken. How do we fix it?
What is the optimum price for the new ____?
What would happen if the loan approval process degraded by 50 percent?
Do I have the right number of sales professionals?

The topic of this book—applying science to business—sounds like a very different and intriguing way to look at the corporate domain of challenges, and it is. Data science and analytics have provided us with better tools than ever before for creating innovative solutions to today's complex problems—the media is full of stories of intelligent business applications converging on whole industries.

It is no accident that you, the problem solver, and I, the problem-solving thinker, have stumbled upon each other. It all began in the early part of the 1990s. Corporate strategy and decision-making began a subtle but fundamental shift, in part due to the advent of personal computers and spreadsheet software and their collective role in bringing beginner-level analytics to the masses. Earlier corporate planning was obsessed with *prediction*. Executive teams worked really hard to predict the future, most often based on pure intuition, then aligned the company to this predicted future.

For an example of the old approach, look no further than the automotive industry in the United States. Economists in firms in the industry created elaborate forecasts of automobile sales, by brand and category, which in turn set in motion an irreversible configuration of the firm to produce to the predicted level. The energy, airline, and shipbuilding industries all mimic this practice to a degree.

It turns out that predicting the future is really, really hard and that in spite of the models showing results with four-decimal-point accuracy, many of these predictions were significantly wrong. There were some spectacular failures splashed across the headlines, but I suspect there were also many less spectacular mini-failures that wasted countless billions of dollars in shareholder value that you never heard about.

The good news

There has never been a better time to apply scientific thinking to business problems. Today, a tailwind of technological developments enables us to do things that were impractical or infeasible even as recently as five years ago. Here are just a few of those developments:

1. **We have access to data as never before**. Data is the fuel of any scientific investigation, and for many years the poor quality or lack of tracking basic data about an organization hindered analytics. Today, most organizations of any size and seriousness have put in place information systems that naturally accumulate accurate data.

2. **Science is better**. I don't mean that science is of higher quality now (although it probably is), but rather that methods in

science that were once considered arcane and purely academic, such as game theory and machine learning, are now finding their way into practical application in business.

3. **Unstoppable rise in computing power.** Computers are the workhorse of modern science these days, and as they get faster and more capable, we reap the benefits. Problems once considered intractable are now practical.

4. **The Web.** The Internet has given us a means to collaborate quickly and inexpensively with a vast array of stakeholders tied to the problem.

It seems that senior leaders in the past era were lulled into the security of knowing that business the next year was simply an incremental change over business this year. That may have held true at one time, but the sea change in corporate life these days is most certainly characterized by dramatic increases in complexity. Competition, for example, could be weak or strong or anywhere in between. Regulatory pressure, weak or strong or anywhere in between. The economy...one could go on and on about the number of "degrees of freedom," but the end result is the same—a very complex picture of thousands, maybe hundreds of thousands of plausible futures before us. Incremental prediction in this climate is doomed to failure.

And so it came to pass that the prediction focus yielded to a more modern view of corporate strategy—an about-face that starts with the admission that we cannot predict the future, but we can create *robustness*. To be robust is to hold up under a wide variety of conditions; therefore, the test of any strategy asks: Does it succeed *relatively* well in, say, 800 out of 1,000 plausible futures versus another strategy that may succeed *remarkably* well, but in only 2 out of 1,000 futures? Clearly, the rational person would choose the former over the latter, but my own personal experience is that, blind to an analysis such as this, leaders often are unintentionally deceived by limited data to pick the latter. Many of the headline-grabbing stories of corporate failure can be traced back to a lack of understanding of robustness among decision-makers.

But how can we possibly test thousands of yet-to-happen futures? Assessing one's corporate strategy across 1,000 or 10,000 or 100,000 futures cannot be done by the average human. Here is where you and I have connected.

In a word, the answer is: models.

By creating a computer-based replica of the system at hand—be it a corporation, a team, or a process—we have taken a step toward the automation of our analysis of any system. Computer-based models, built and managed properly, are quite adept at considering thousands or even hundreds of thousands of hypothetical future states of a system by calculating all of the outcomes.

This book is about using models to solve a wide range of business problems using data, math, and methodically applied processes. This first chapter discusses how to start the process of building models. Software developers often use the term "Hello World" to describe a first step in learning a language by creating a trivially simple program, say to output a string "Hello, World!". We will do the same here for model building, but using words and pictures.

Say the words "computer model," and you often conjure up a mental image of an extremely elaborate tapestry of mathematical equations—evoking memories of your college professor completely filling a classroom blackboard. Yet models do not have to be complex. In fact, best practice in model building suggests that one should build models just complex enough to answer the question, but go no further.

The Kindest Cut of All

In science we use a principle known as Occam's razor to support the idea of investigating new phenomena using models that make the fewest possible assumptions. Models, the reasoning goes, can always be made more complex in any situation. The more useful ones are those that are simple enough to be testable.

A model doesn't even have to be computer software. If you draw two circles on a piece of paper and label one "income tax rate" and the other "GDP," then draw an arrow from one to the other, congratulations: You have now built a model, one that asserts a relationship between two measurable variables. In the next chapters we will show you how to effectively and efficiently build much more sophisticated models as a means of generating insight into complex problems. The point is that a model is at its core an abstract representation of the real system, laid down in a format—a diagram, computer code, an equation—that can be shared with and understood by others. *Anyone* can build models at some level, and that is important because doing so is a fundamental step in connecting your problem to the tools that science can offer you.

Throughout this book I will refer to our goal as *problem solving*. Yet the word "problem" itself is a problem—it implies something negative. You are in a jam, and you need help with a problem. Some situations are like that, but my definition is much broader. Meeting the challenge of a new product line to be introduced next year, figuring out how to make a system work 10 percent better, and managing an organization that is growing beyond expectations are all examples of what science would call problems, simply because they need systematic solutions, not because something bad is going on that needs to be fixed.

How Science Looks at Solving Problems

Science views the challenge of any discovery through the lens of the scientific method, the early roots of which can be traced back to Aristotle's teachings on deductive reasoning in the fourth century BCE. The scientific method that we know today followed a circuitous route through history, with many contributors from René Descartes to Francis Bacon. Twenty-five centuries of evolution later, we now have a widely accepted, well-tested, and universal structure for scientific investigation. More than likely, you were introduced to it quite early in your formal education.

There are as many subtle interpretations of the scientific method as there are scientists, but generally speaking, the steps include in Table 1.1.

Table 1.1 Steps of the scientific method

Observation	I observe activity and events around me that require an explanation
Research	I study known information about the systems in place
Hypothesis	I create a point of view to explain the events in the form of a question to be proved or disproved
Prediction	I predict what will happen to a system given controlled changes to it
Experimentation	I make tests to the system or a representation of it
Conclusion	I use all preceding steps to devise a conclusive explanation

We have arrived at the very first lesson that science teaches us—use a thoughtful, stepwise means to attack complex problems. Notice that the scientific method has a number of steps before we get to the actual solution development stage and that all of these emphasize thinking about and defining *the problem*. In my 30 years of working with corporate teams of every shape and size, I have found that the common thread in the failure to get to a solution was not in the selection of the right technology or the application of the wrong math. *It was trying to solve the wrong problem.* Everyone carries around with them a "mental model" of what the problem is and the words used to describe it. Until you elaborate that problem for all to see, which is the purpose of the first three steps above, it is impossible to get a shared understanding among all of the contributors. "We know what the problem is, let's just get to it" is a common reaction I get from companies I work with. However, it is important for you to resist shortcuts to the scientific method, as all of the steps are in place for a reason.

What do I mean by the *wrong* problem? It can take many forms, but the wrong problem is most often confusion between cause and effect.

I once worked with an airline that was in substantial tension with its pilots' union. The union had a history of granting concessions when times were tough and asking for wage increases when the company was doing well. The airline had just reached a point of profitability after a long turn-around effort and needed to retain earnings for its next stage of growth. The union's insistence on sharing the success (through wage increases) was legitimate, as the pilots had played a key role in the turn-around, but was in conflict with the company's growth strategy. The company asked me to run some calculations to devise a wage level that would just minimally satisfy the pilots but retain enough investment income to fuel the growth plan.

I did run the calculations for the company, but I also pointed out that we were not actually solving the problem. The *real* problem was the unhealthy relationship between the company and its pilots, in which wage increases and decreases were poorly timed to the financial needs of the company, creating earnings volatility that severely hampered operations and strategy. Solving the problem of this particular cycle would not prevent us from having to devise yet another solution in the next cycle. Rather, we had to rework the structure of the relationship to solve the problem in a sustainable way.

The conversation about solving the more foundational problem led us to devise a package of interventions that, in effect, made the pilots shareholders in the company. In doing so, we created a completely different structural relationship between the company and its pilots—one that established a shared incentive around earnings, resulting in stable earnings, and in turn a path toward manageable growth of the whole system.

To an outsider, this solution may sound extraordinarily simple. You might conclude that you could have come up with a solution like that without an elaborate process using models or data. That may be partially true, but from the inside of an airline what you see is an incredibly complex, dynamic environment in which it is difficult to isolate any one part of the operations to put meaningful interventions in place. The models allowed us to create just such an isolation by abstracting the real, messy, noisy system into one that provided a clean perspective into a very specific part of that system.

Secondly, in an airline you do not simply try an intervention, even a straightforward one, without extensively testing it first, and the models provided us a means to consider not just the direct effects but the unintended consequences as well.

The wrong problem can also mean the right problem at the wrong level of granularity. Let me offer an example:

You: "George I just won the lottery, and I want to buy some stocks on the stock market. What stock should I buy?"

George: "What do you consider a good stock?"

You: "Oh, I don't know…perhaps something that earns me 10 percent on my investment."

George: "OK, I'll work on it."

And so off I go to conduct research, build models, crunch some numbers. I come back two weeks later.

George: "OK, I found this stock—ABC Company, and according to my analysis it will give you an 11.5 percent return."

You: "Great thanks. I'll place the order today."

I gave an appropriate answer to the question that was posed—what stock will yield about a 10 percent return. Now let's try an alternative. Instead of coming back in two weeks, I take six months and come back with this statement:

George: "OK, I found this stock—ABC Company, and according to my analysis it will give you an 11.5289875924987587 percent return."

I have most certainly answered your question, but I have *overmodeled* the problem. I see this in my own work with companies all of the time, constantly overmodeling problems with a perceived need for extreme detail in their mental models. By navigating your problem through the rigor of the scientific method, you will elaborate the right level of granularity and avoid these kinds of errors.

The Scientific Method Is Not Just for Science

The scientific method was designed to allow scientists to conduct formal investigations of nature. Most of you are not scientists, and you have no special interest in nature, but in principle you are conducting a similar formal investigation into a business problem. Therefore, some level of adaptation of the scientific method for our use in business problem solving is fair game, and it begins with organizing ourselves around the three principal components of analysis, then concludes with the analysis itself. Figure 1.1 shows a scientific process that is well suited to problem solving.

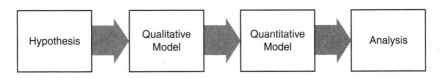

Figure 1.1   The scientific method adapted for problem solving

1. The *hypothesis* is a clear, simple restatement of the problem
2. The *qualitative model* is a depiction of the underlying story behind the hypothesis
3. The *quantitative model* is the software that performs the calculations and generates a view to the result
4. *Analysis* is using the quantitative model over and over with different inputs to conduct a series of experiments.

Let us take each one of these steps in turn and describe its features.

Hypothesis

There is no more critical step in the whole of model building than the development of the hypothesis. It sets the tone of the model to come, and governs the design in the same way that a constitution governs a country. It pays to take time to get the hypothesis right.

A hypothesis should consist of two parts—a curve or set of curves over time, followed by a summary statement. Let me illustrate with an example.

I was once asked by a board member to model a merger his company was executing. Here was our initial dialogue on the problem:

> *Board Member*: "Wall Street doesn't understand our logic in this merger and have discounted our market value as a result. We need to show them our thinking, educate them on the complex advantages of putting these two companies together so that they will correctly value the combination."
>
> *George*: "OK, you need to describe a merger. So what is the problem?"
>
> *Board Member*: "The analysts don't see the need for the merger. On top of that, they fear the costs of integrating the two companies will outweigh the benefits. They would have preferred that we carry on with our core business as is."
>
> *George*: "The analysts are smart people. Perhaps they are right?"
>
> *Board Member*: "They could be, and we don't discount their view. We have a sound core business and will be relatively profitable even if we don't merge. But look, every successful merger goes through the same cycle—incur the difficult costs of integration, followed by a larger, more profitable company coming out the other end."
>
> *George*: "And you've already shared your reasoning through the data you have."
>
> *Board Member*: "Yes, we have, many times. We just feel like they are missing the other part of the story—our justification based on how we see the company can be configured once the merger

happens—because the story is complicated and mired in company-specific jargon."

The critical skill in building a good hypothesis is in allowing your thinking to rise above the specific, parochial details of the problem to glean the "meta" problem in play. Some call this the signal-to-noise challenge, deciphering the tiny salient aspects of the problem from the vast ocean of information that matters far less at this stage. So let us now apply a ruthless filter to the dialogue you've just seen. Let us take stock of what we know:

1. There are two possible futures here: one with the merger and one without the merger.
2. In the merger scenario, there is a worse-before-better cycle.
3. The company has to prove that a far more profitable company results from the merger

Let us now start to put these key ideas into a proper hypothesis form.

Step 1. *Show the future with no merger at all.* Our board member said that without the merger, the business was sound—"relatively profitable." When I pressed him further on that, he said that the company could reasonably be expected to perform at the rate of the general economy, which at the time was growing slowly but steadily.

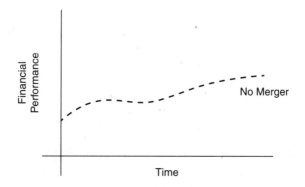

Figure 1.2 The base case

Step 2. *Overlay the alternative scenario of the merger.* The board member described the initial costs related to integration, followed by a more profitable combined company.

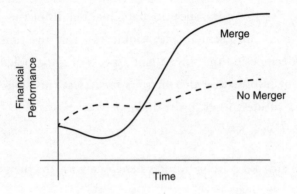

Figure 1.3 Adding the merger effect

Step 3. *Make a statement to be proven* (or disproven).

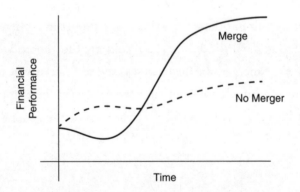

This merger, after absorbing some near-term integration costs, will result in a much more profitable company in the long run.

Figure 1.4 The final hypothesis

There you have it…our working hypothesis.

"But wait," you might say, "two curves and a sentence? Is that it?"

It is true that this hypothesis is surprisingly simple, but when you look closely, there is quite a bit going on here. The curves suggest that the future company without the merger will follow a "steady as she goes" path. It also suggests that there is in fact an integration cost penalty and it is "yay big." There is a time out in the future at which the curves meet—a break-even point. There is a reset of profitability to a new level. There is a flattening of that merge curve that suggests that once the new profitability plane is reached, there must be new sources of growth. Those "two curves and a sentence" are establishing quite a few assertions.

But what about dates, values, amounts? Remember what the board member said: our story is "complicated and mired in company-specific jargon." The leadership team working on the merger lived in a world of just such details, and followed a natural inclination to include all of those details to help their audience understand. In fact, they did precisely the opposite—the story became untellable, as it was burdened with all of that information. Simplicity equals clarity. There will be plenty of opportunities to carefully weave numbers and facts into the hypothesis as we get to the qualitative model stage.

A good hypothesis sets the stage for further analysis by cutting away all of the unnecessary details to get to the single most important question to be answered. A great hypothesis begs more questions than it answers: Is it really true that the core business will do "just OK" without the merger? How big is the integration dip? How high is the new profitability plane? When will the merger reach break even against the nonmerger scenario? How specifically will we measure "financial performance"?

I often find that the debate that is stimulated regarding the hypothesis is as valuable to companies as is the hypothesis itself. Teams begin to ask themselves these very questions, prompted by the process of putting it together and writing something down on paper. This idea really hit home for me during a particular working session for a major retailer to solve an issue related to predictions of store sales. The executive sponsor pulled me aside and told me, "George, I don't even care if your model works. I'm just happy that this handful of experts critical to our business are in one room and writing down how they think."

Notice that the example hypothesis is completely silent on any of the aspects of "how." No solution is presented whatsoever; rather, the hypothesis suggests simply that there *is* a solution and what form that solution will take. This is a critical design feature of hypotheses—you must suggest that there exists a solution, but go no further to define a particular solution.

The hypothesis is a springboard to the analysis—what the model will be asked to do. Clearly, in this case the model must serve as a replica of the company in software, then express the merger and nonmerger outcomes. The case for the merger is "proven" if the output of the model matches the hypothesis.

Qualitative Model

The hypothesis delineates the problem, and the qualitative model begins the process of elaborating the system that underlies that problem. As the name suggests, qualitative modeling is light on numbers but heavy on pictures sprinkled with a few words.

Our job is to explain the behavior of the system that gave rise to the "curves" in the hypothesis, and we will do that by constructing a series of graphical depictions that tell a cogent story about the system.

Qualitative model development is one of the most creative parts of our adaptation of the scientific method, as it is up to the builder to choose how to represent the system graphically. There is no rigid format for how that is done—it could be *any* kind of diagram, from causal loops to process flow, or perhaps even a form bespoke to the system at hand. That does not mean there are no "wrong" qualitative models that do a poor job of giving the audience a clear, simple, and complete representation of the system in a natural way.

Creativity makes it difficult to provide specific guidance to you on how to build qualitative models. Rather, I will set down a few principles to follow that will increase your chances of success.

Ask yourself about the nature of the system. Is it factory-like with a number of sequential steps? Is it marked by continuous flows and activity, like ants building an anthill? Does it evolve from one state to another over time? Is there any short-term behavior that gives rise to a longer term behavior? Is it a system that is supposed to work in one way but works in a different way that must be corrected?

Before you begin drawing, ask yourself these kinds of questions to get to the core attributes of the system at hand. And don't be shy about reaching out for metaphors and analogs. If the system resembles a river, a beehive, a traffic signal—these are extremely useful ways to cut the parochial details from the actual system to get to its essential features.

Now begin to draw—I recommend doing this by hand on paper as you are learning. If the system is sequential in nature, make the steps flow left to right across the page. If it needs to show a contrast between two states, show one state on the left and one to the right. The style of the system that emerged from your basic questions about its nature should drive the way you represent it in a picture. Continue until you have covered the story from end to end before you critique and refine.

Text plays an important role in qualitative models, but it must be used sparingly. Problems become intractable inside of organizations because they are shrouded in lengthy, incomprehensible text. In your qualitative model, use text primarily as labels, short explanatory phrases, and titles.

How-to: How to practice hypothesis and qualitative model development

The front end of the scientific method is challenging for anyone. I recommend lots of practice, as would be appropriate for any complex skill with subtle aspects. Here's how:

1. Pick an article from any newspaper or newsmagazine. The front-page stories tend to be the best candidates.
2. Read the story carefully. As you read, think of the structure the journalist is trying to convey. Who are the key actors, objects?

Is something unfolding over time? Is there a chain of causes and effects here? It is sometimes helpful to highlight or circle key nouns and verbs.

3. Create a hypothesis from the story. What few curves over time can convey the issue at hand?

4. Make guesses on what the journalist, and the subject matter experts interviewed would have to say about the system. Use your guesses to build a qualitative model.

5. Compare your finished exhibits to the story. Is your representation of the problem clean and clear to someone other than yourself? Could someone get the same level of understanding (or better) from viewing your exhibits alone as opposed to reading the story?

You will be far from perfect in your practice, but the end result isn't in the quality of the exhibits—it is how your brain begins to grasp the process of taking a story in one form—lots of words and even some noise—moving that story to a systematized form appropriate for assimilation into a model. Over time, your brain will begin to do this instinctively. You will never look at written articles the same way again.

Quantitative Model

Moving from qualitative model to quantitative model is akin to constructing a house from the blueprints. The qualitative model is your central guide on how the model software is to be created. Your qualitative model should be free of any language-specific aspects, allowing the developer (even if that is you) the freedom to create the code in any language that is suitable to the application.

One of the first issues you will want to think about is the overall technical architecture of the model. The most common and universal structure for software models is shown in Figure 1.5.

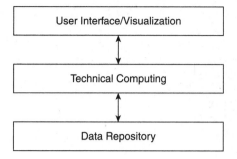

Figure 1.5 The general technical architecture of a model

At its foundation there is a repository for holding all of the necessary data to be used by the model. Next, there is a technical computing environment for describing and executing the calculations and logic chain. Finally, there is the user interface/visualization layer that is exposed to the users, allowing for interaction and analysis. Software professionals collectively refer to this structure as a "stack" due to its vertical arrangement.

The boundaries of the layers are the interfaces between systems. The technical computing environment must be capable of selectively reading in data from the repository. At the same time, the user must be "served" sensible visualizations through controls on the user interface.

With the architecture completed, we generally start with the design of the data. Your qualitative model blueprint implies certain objects to be known by the system. Say you are working on a supply chain model involving the movement of parts via truck from a warehouse to a set of retailers scattered across a region. Your simulated world will have trucks, a warehouse, some orders, retailers. For each of these objects, you will want to know some things that are specific to that object—the capacity of the truck and its costs per mile, the lat/long location of the warehouse, which retailer an order is destined for. By simply imagining the world that must be created as a replica of the real world, you will have an excellent start on the data design. As data is aligned to tables, you will want the table name to take on the object name, and the attributes of the object to form its associated fields. While there are many ways to structure a data design, Figure 1.6 shows an example format that we often use in our practice.

Sales Planning Data Model

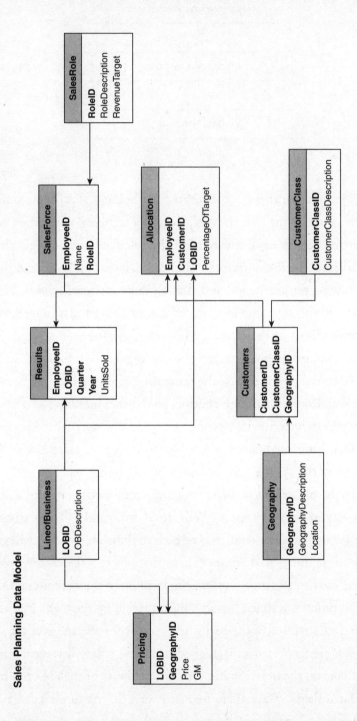

Figure 1.6 Example data model

This format allows us to use the background field of the table's title block to color code tables in cases where we wish to categorize them in some way.

Chapter 3 covers the entire aspect of data.

Sidebar: The right and wrong ways to use Excel

Microsoft Excel is often the first software system analysts will reach for when called to develop a model, not because it is the best tool for the objective, but rather because it is freely available and is perhaps the only numerical application around that requires little to no training. Worse yet, spreadsheets that start at a simple level tend to evolve over time into enormous, interconnected forests of calculations and data, yet the developer continues to stay with spreadsheets long after its practical limits have been exceeded.

The spreadsheet is a perfectly fine tool for a certain limited class of work: collecting, filtering, and cleansing data, testing calculations, entering data for models, building small prototype calculations, and validating model results. It is NOT, however, suitable for large system development because of one fundamental feature: spreadsheets do not clearly separate *calculations* from *data*. A casual user looking at a spreadsheet cannot determine which cells are formula based and which are simple numbers or text in a cell. Therefore, the logic and flow of the model are not obvious to anyone but the developer. Furthermore, spreadsheets offer a very limited gallery of visualizations (and many of those visualizations violate good practice in information design).

It is certainly possible to organize a spreadsheet in a very systematic manner using tabs, colored regions, explanatory text, and well-placed macros, and one should use these features. In any case, the fundamental structure of spreadsheets does NOT lend itself well to substantive model development for the kinds of business problems we are discussing here. We will discuss a range of practical and effective software tools in chapter 5.

Analysis

The completion of the quantitative model is the gateway to analysis, in which we use the model to conduct a range of experiments. The experiments are closely aligned to the hypothesis we constructed at the outset of the project. Our goal: can we prove or disprove the hypothesis using various runs of the model, each run a change in the input variables representing a hypothetical configuration of the real system?

Scientists use the term *controlled experiments*, whereby a particular aspect of the system under study is changed, all other conditions held constant. The change in the outcome can therefore be isolated to the single change that was made.

Let's use a simple example. Suppose you have a working hypothesis that the addition of two more service technicians would dramatically improve the output of an auto repair shop. You create a computer simulation model of the shop and all of its processes for repairing a batch of cars. Proving (or disproving) that hypothesis requires a minimum of two runs of the model, one with the current number of technicians, and one with the current number plus two. All other conditions—the number of cars, coming in, the time to repair particular vehicles, the layout of the shop—remain exactly the same, hence the term "controlled" experiment. It would be fair to say that any difference in outcome—in this case the overall throughput per unit of time—between the two experiments can be attributed to the addition of the two technicians since that was the only difference introduced in the two cases. This is the advantage of a simulated world, as it is rare that we can so easily control such factors from one point in time to the next.

It is likely that you already have a strong basis for experiments right there in your organization. If this is an important problem that has been around for a while, many people touched by it have suggested theories they wish to test. "What if we tried ___?" "What would happen if we did___?" and other common refrains. These are ideal candidates for experiments to try, even multiple experiment ideas in concert with one another if not mutually exclusive.

It is important to draw a distinction between a controlled experiment and the overall goal of the project that led us to create a simulation model. In our auto repair example, perhaps the goal was to "find the best configuration of the shop to ensure the most profitable operation." Note that this is quite different from a single controlled experiment in which the analyst is trying to understand the effect, positive or negative, of one surgical change in the system, implying the need to run many controlled experiments for all of the possible changes to answer the overarching goal question. In our own work it is not uncommon to run hundreds of these controlled experiments, at least one for each individual factor plus pairwise combinations of factors. The good news is that most properly built computer simulation models allow a degree of automation so that multiple runs can be executed all at once.

Often you will be asked to evaluate a system that has already been in place for quite some time. The goal is to understand how it works under a variety of conditions and use that knowledge to improve it in some way. For those systems with a history of operation, we often use a technique called *relative analysis.*

Relative analysis uses a time period of past history to isolate a specific *"as is"* behavior of the system—how the system actually behaved over the period of time in question. Going back to our auto repair shop example, we likely have all of the job tickets from last year, the staff schedule each week over that year, the parts inventory—all of the data needed to reconstruct "a year in the life" of the repair shop. Imagine watching a video of the shop across an entire year at 100x speed with a dashboard of key metrics superimposed on the video screen.

Now take that same time frame and transport yourself back in time. Add two more service technicians at the start of the year and see what happens. How did our year-in-the-life change? This is the *"to be"* run of the model. Relative analysis seeks to contrast as-is directly against to-be, where the as-is is an actual piece of historical operation of the system. Often relative analysis makes a more compelling argument for change because the as-is is the real, undisputed behavior of the system. My recommendation is to use relative analysis whenever you have the rare luxury of access to historical performance of the system under study.

The Strategy Matrix

Let us return to our discussion of strategy and robustness at the beginning of this chapter. Recall that we defined the robustness of a system as one that succeeds across many possible futures rather than just a few. In the analysis stage, in which our goal is to help executives understand the implication of a range of strategic alternatives for the organization, we often use a *strategy matrix* to frame the robustness question, as shown in Figure 1.7.

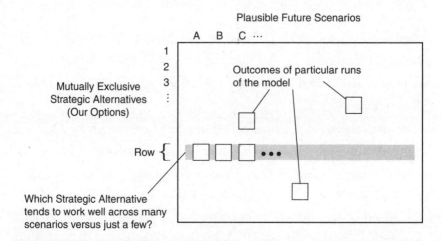

Figure 1.7　The strategy matrix

The strategy matrix is a visual device used to focus on a row-wise comparison of available strategic alternatives. The columns are all of the plausible external scenarios—those exogenous factors (the market, regulations, competitors, nature) that can affect our organization in material ways. Each "cell" in the matrix is a particular simulation model run outcome (which may in turn be a basket of calculated metrics) using the strategic alternative on that row to dictate the inputs to the model against the scenario that is designated by the column. The strategy matrix can be thought of as a home for all of the model-driven experiments relating to the company strategy.

A properly built strategy matrix should have the effect of steering management thinking away from "what is my best/worst/middle of the road outcome?" toward "what can I do to make my organization robust?" This is what simulation models should do—not provide answers on their face, but rather, *cause humans to ask the right questions.*

Key point

It is very important to note that when we finish a modeling exercise, we have achieved much more than simply solving the problem. By working in the ways of science, we have also created a number of artifacts across our four-step process—the hypothesis, the qualitative model, the quantitative model, the data—that *tell the story* of our thinking along the way, with clear, simple documents and diagrams illustrating the terms and concepts of the subject. In many ways these artifacts are as valuable as the solution itself, because having a language and medium for problem solving is an institutional capability that *every* organization should seek.

Chapter Summary

Problem solving is one of the most important unrecognized activities we do every day, no matter what sector of the economy we come from. To do it better, we draw lessons from the 24 centuries of science that came before us, all conducted under the durable framework known as the scientific method.

A modern adaptation of the scientific method involves moving a problem through four steps: hypothesis, qualitative model, quantitative model, and analysis. The result is new insight into the problem's solution through the lens of objective experimentation. Equally important are the physical artifacts of documents and diagrams that are created along the way, enabling the solver to tell the story of how the problem was examined and the solution came to be.

Now that you fully understand the process for solving problems scientifically, it is time to turn our attention to a crucial step that occurs just after the qualitative model but before the quantitative model—the selection of a mathematical method upon which to base the quantitative model. It is a thought process that involves mapping the properties of the problem to the features of a mathematical method or methods. The next chapter will offer some practical guidelines for choosing methods that are appropriate to the problem.

CHAPTER 2

Methods and Madness

Have you ever watched a car race? A critical moment occurs when the car pulls into the pits and the crew goes to work. The team springs into action to replace tires, clean the windshield, and assist the driver. In seconds the car is back on the track.

Think about what just happened in slow motion. Each crew member had the tools and the knowledge to apply perform a specific job. The person responsible for the left rear tire, for instance, had just such a tire in hand, along with the drill needed to remove the old tire and mount the new one. The function was precisely matched to the need, and the result was an astonishingly effective upgrade to the car's performance.

Our effectiveness in solving business problems arises in part from our ability to use tools that are precisely matched to each problem. We can be very fast with a wrench, but that is useless if the job needs a screwdriver. Confusion sets in when we use the wrench, unnaturally, as a screwdriver. The vital skill in problem solving is recognizing the attributes of the problem at hand and mapping those attributes thoughtfully to mathematical methods that are appropriate to them. In this chapter I introduce you to a range of methods as well as their strengths and special features.

Key Point: Dumbing down

It seems so logical, doesn't it, to just match the problem to the method or the tool to the problem. Yet in my own practice, I have seen many organizations limit the range of tools and methods available to their people, primarily through the accessibility of their software. "Just use Excel, because...uh...that's what we have on our desktops" or "IT just invested millions in this new app, so we were told we had to use it for any business problems in a certain category." In effect, we have bureaucratized something that should be a carefully executed craft. It is no wonder that organizations are struggling to solve thorny problems these days in spite of their armies of smart people.

Any business problem worth the time and attention of an organization deserves to be solved free of any artificial corporate constraints, such as arbitrary software standards. Companies should be seeking to create a culture of experimentation. Such a culture requires a wide range of tools for scientific investigation.

Chapter 1 introduced the problem-solving process:

A disciplined sequence of steps designed to guide the problem solver methodically through the problem's solution. Candidate methods are introduced in the qualitative modeling step, and implemented in the quantitative modeling step. Therefore is it is important to note the critical transition...

There is a critical transition from the qualitative model to the quantitative model. The qualitative model is the blueprint of the system that lies at the heart of the problem. The quantitative model is the analytical mechanism that will be used to understand the system, often by re-creating some part of the system in code. The qualitative model therefore becomes the guidebook by which the quantitative model is built.

Quantitative model development is akin to constructing a laboratory—a place in which to conduct experiments. Any laboratory contains numerous pieces of physical equipment—test instruments, fixtures, tools. Our job is to create the software-based analogues to these objects as a means to test our specimen—the problem itself and, more specifically, the data related to the problem.

Done well, the qualitative model shows the attributes of the problem: Does the system unfold over time? Is there a sequence of steps in a system?

What are the knowns and the unknowns? Our focus is to choose the underlying *methods* for the quantitative model that are match these attributes.

For example, a system with lots of local interacting actors, such as traffic on a set of roads, is likely well suited to an agent-based approach. A process, such as the approval of a loan or the financial reconciliation of a transaction, speaks to a flow model. A risk-based future investment decision possibly calls for the Monte Carlo simulation. Do not worry if these terms are unfamiliar—we will be covering these and more later in the chapter. The key point is that there is a correct method (or methods) for every problem, a method that maps to the features of the problem itself.

A method is a set of algorithms—steps in a recipe, if you like—united under an overall approach to transform input data in one form into results in another form. A proper-fitting method is achieved when the chosen method (or methods) illuminates the problem sufficiently so that we can draw conclusions about it, in much the same way as a piece of test equipment in a real laboratory reveals information about the test specimen.

What are all of these mathematical methods at our disposal? What do they do? Do we have to be mathematicians to understand them?

If you have ever used a spreadsheet, you are already using a mathematical method. Most spreadsheets are structured to solve a chain of formulas for an unknown value, given a set of known values. That's called algebra. Surprisingly, a wide range of even complex problems can be solved using simple algebra, so you already have a leg up on one of the foundational methods without thinking of yourself as a mathematician. But just as every building cannot be built with a hammer alone, every problem cannot be solved with just one method. We need to understand a wide range of methods if we are to tackle any conceivable problem that comes our way. This chapter explains some very powerful (but accessible-to-nonmathematicians) methods that will be a valuable addition to your problem-solving arsenal.

The list of mathematical methods that one may use when solving problems presented in this chapter is by no means a complete. Even if it were at the time of publication, new methods are being developed every day. Please check the companion website at www.business-laboratory.com/profitfromscience for the latest thoughts on emerging methods and tools. In the meantime, I have selected methods for discussion here that have proven to be particularly effective and accessible and that cover a wide range of problem types.

My plan is to introduce you to these methods in a way that creates familiarity but stops short of a comprehensive "how-to" on each—that would require a complete book in itself. There are many resources to draw upon to go deeper into each method, and I encourage you to do so in the next logical progression of your proficiency in solving complex problems.

Simulation Modeling

Often we want to create an abstract replica of a system in the computer so that we can experiment with it in ways that are difficult, expensive, or downright dangerous to do in a real-world system. The process of crafting the replica is called simulation modeling, and the replica itself is often referred to as the simulation.

Let's take the example of an airline—an industry with which I have worked on occasion. Now let's say that you wanted to see what the cost effect might be of changing a few of the routes in the system, say, by flying from Chicago to Philadelphia to St. Louis and back, as opposed to the reverse of that loop. Now, you could order the airline to change the route on a particular day and measure the cost of that run versus the cost of the status quo, but of course that would be quite disruptive to the airline's operations. A better approach is to break down the airline's functions on this particular route within a *mathematical representation* of it, with sufficient realism to show the cost implications of before versus after.

Keep in mind that you don't need a perfect replica of every aspect of the airline to determine the cost difference between the two route options. In fact, this is a very fundamental principle of simulation modeling that we first introduced in chapter 1—we should model to a level of realism sufficient to answer the hypothesis question but go no further. We could incorporate the aircraft fleet, the prices of the tickets, and competitors' flights—real-world features, to be sure, but features that are more or less irrelevant to the hypothesis question. Time and again, the failure of models to meet the expectations of the audience comes from *overmodeling* the system at hand. In part this stems from the fact that many people live in the details of the real-world systems that they manage. Some people spend entire careers devoted to a narrow set of details. To these people who often are the subject matter experts in an organization, *any* absence of detail renders the model useless. You must resist this overcomplication at every turn by arguing for *sensible abstraction* of the system.

The goal in simulation modeling is to create an artificial world that behaves like the real system. This is done by creating analogous software objects. Each object has two aspects to it: its class—what kind of thing it is—and its instance—which *particular* thing it is. Consider the example in Figure 2.1, a car. The block defines the class of car (title of the block). Every car, no matter what kind it is, is presumed to have these attributes: a license plate number, a color, a make (manufacturer), and a model number (body of the block).

From the class as a template, we create individual instances of cars—my car, my neighbor's car, John's car—all of the car instances we need as

Figure 2.1   The car class

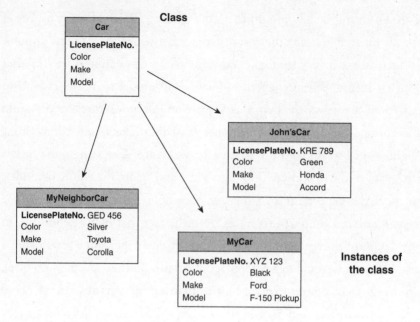

Figure 2.2 The class and its instances

shown in Figure 2.2. We can then go further to create traffic lights, pedestrians—all of the different classes of objects that comprise the actors in the simulated world.

Now that we have created all of the actors, the next task is to create the stage upon which they will act. That means roads, signage, cities, and the like—the "static" objects that form the environment in which the actors move and interact.

Finally, we need to set the scene in motion. A master mechanism in code initializes all of the objects, reads a set of parameters, and simulates time. It then paces and broadcasts time for all the objects that are busy implementing their behavioral rules. A complete cycle of the model from start to finish is called a *run*.

Typically simulation models exhibit a scorecard of metrics, showing the vital signs of how the system is performing as the simulation runs. The scorecard allows the user to observe system performance, perhaps comparing that performance to another run that has a different set of parameters. See the example of a natural gas exploration model, shown in Figure 2.3.

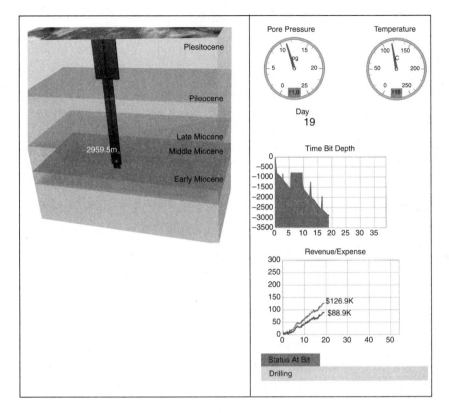

Figure 2.3 Simulation example

Simulation is ideal for those cases in which experimenting with the real system is impractical, infeasible, or downright dangerous. Say we want to understand how traffic flows by constantly moving a traffic light from one block to the next. What is unthinkable in the real world is completely practical in a simulation—just tell the simulation that the traffic light object sits here versus there, and rerun the model to find out what the implications are. The simulation becomes a "laboratory" of sorts in which what-if questions can be investigated quantitatively.

I describe simulation modeling first because it is what I call super-method—many of the methods we discuss next *can be used as part of this process*. In other words, simulation modeling is a platform for the integration of many other methods, including optimization, agent-based modeling, and flow modeling.

Optimization

Optimization is the second cousin of simulation, in that it also involves a replica of a system under study. However, instead of the user's changing the parameters of a model to run under varying conditions, in optimization we allow the computer to do that for us—to seek an optimal value of one of the outputs.

Let's say you run a furniture factory that makes only three products: chairs, tables, and desks. Each item has a different selling price, and each item also has a different number of labor hours that go into making it, along with a different amount of wood needed.

You have a fixed amount of wood and a fixed number of workers to make products. The goal: select the number of chairs, tables, and desks in a way that maximizes the profit for your factory.

At first glance, it seems like a trivial question. Why not just get out a spreadsheet, create the chain of formulas for profit, start trying values for the number of chairs, tables, and desks, and keep trying until you get the highest profit? First of all, this *seemingly innocent* problem has thousands of plausible answers. Second, what if tomorrow your business partner comes into the factory and tells you that you have 10 percent less wood than you had first counted? You will have to start guessing all over again.

The right answer for even this simple problem is to employ an optimization model so that the computer does the hard work of iterating across the thousands of possibilities very quickly to arrive at the final, optimal answer.

All optimization models require three components:

1. *An objective function.* This is the way in which you tell the computer when you have reached the final, optimum answer. "Maximize profit" could be an objective, as could "minimize distance traveled."
2. *A set of constraints.* You must bind the solutions by giving the model a set of rules to maintain. In our furniture example, "Consume no more than X amount of wood" would be a constraint that makes sure

the model does not choose a solution that uses more wood on hand. You might also put in a constraint of "consume no more than Y labor hours" in a similar way.

3. *Variables.* These are the items that the computer will change in its relentless drive toward finding the optimum. For the furniture example, these are the numbers of tables, chairs, and desks.

Even if you don't plan to create optimization models of your own, it is helpful to recognize the structure of optimization models so that you can ensure that the right elements are brought to bear on the solution, as in "do we have all of the right constraints built in? Is the objective function the correct one?"

Systems Thinking/System Dynamics

One school of thought in analytics is that structures of systems—the visible and the invisible—drive the behaviors we see in system interactions. Therefore, to understand observed behavior, we must first understand the underlying structure that underpins it. This line of reasoning gave birth to the science of systems thinking and its quantitative counterpart, system dynamics.

The core principle here is that complex systems are made up of cause-and-effect linkages. The health of the economy influences consumption of goods, which drives consumer prices...and so on. Moreover, these linkages are not linear, but in fact turn on themselves in a loop, which is referred to as a feedback loop. Feedback loops can be of two varieties—reinforcing, as in a virtuous or vicious cycle, or balancing, as in a steering wheel's keeping a car in the middle of the lane. Systems theory holds that all systems, no matter how simple or complex, can be represented through a series of interlocking loops.

The language of systems thinking is the *causal loop diagram*, a syntax for describing the relationships between elements of a system in the form of feedback loops. Fundamentally there are two types of relationships between any two variables, as shown in Figure 2.4.

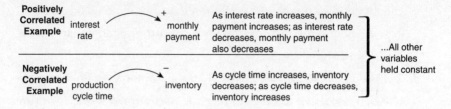

Figure 2.4 Two types of relationships between variables

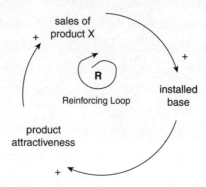

Figure 2.5 A reinforcing loop

Now when we chain relationships together in their logical sequence, we see loops beginning to form, as shown in Figure 2.5.

This is what is known as a reinforcing loop, which describes a structure that gives rise to virtuous (or vicious) cycles of behavior. In the sales example, as shown in Figure 2.6, sales made in the market increase the installed base of the product, which in turn raises the attractiveness of the product to buyers, leading to even more sales (note that the converse case of declining sales triggering a shrinkage in the installed base and so on is *also* true and is supported by this same model).

The other type of feedback loop is the balancing loop, in which the system exhibits an equilibrium-seeking behavior, as shown in Figure 2.7. The presence of a large number of predators, say, can drive down the population of prey. Over time, this starves the predators, reducing their population. Fewer predators then leads to an increase in prey population and so on, in an oscillation around the balance of predator/prey populations.

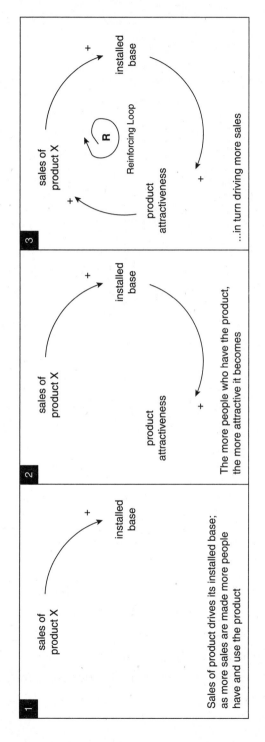

Figure 2.6 Construction of a feedback loop step by step

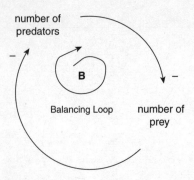

Figure 2.7 A balancing loop

These are both very simple examples, to be sure. A complete model might consist of a number of feedback loop structures that at times share variables across them. Systems thinking seeks to understand the behavior of systems we observe at the surface level by re-creating the structure below those systems that give rise to the readily observed performance.

Systems thinking is excellent for problems of insight, which involves understanding the behavior of a particular system that seems difficult to describe in simple, intuitive ways.

Even if you do not intend to use systems thinking directly in your work, I highly recommend a working knowledge of it as it is a valuable skill that applies to many modeling disciplines.

Agent-Based Models

Agent-based modeling extends the notion of simulation modeling that we described earlier. The subtle differences occur in how the software objects interact with each other in the simulated world.

The objective of agent-based modeling is to create an environment in which actors ("agents") over time engage with other actors and with the environment itself through the execution of local agent rules over time. The synthetic world is a software counterpart to a real-world system under study. For example, you may want to study the reaction of crowds to a fire in a building. The agents are the people in the building, while the fire and the building configuration is the environment. Some agents will move rapidly away from the fire and toward the closest exit. Some agents will panic and freeze. Still others will "follow the herd." All of these are examples of rules that are imparted among agents. The collective behavior (how many people got out of the building and in how much time) is the outcome of interest to the analyst.

Agent-based modeling has been used by biologists to study the behavior of ant colonies. Ant colonies are particularly well suited to agent models because it is said that the colonies do very sophisticated collective tasks (foraging for food, building and maintaining nests, recovering from shocks like predators and weather events), while each individual ant is relatively unsophisticated, following a few very simple rules. If ant colonies can thrive, even under attack, how can we build organizations with a network of talent that engages in local tasks that add up to a beneficial, collective result? As our human organizations become much larger, more distributed, and more complex, it will no longer be possible to manage from the top. The practical alternative is to manage by "designing" local rules that create a positive overall outcome. Simulations can show how this works very effectively. In our own work we showed a company in the logistics industry how to build a self-healing supply chain that can withstand shocks from extraordinary weather events, which in the past had always caused substantial problems. Based on the foraging patterns of ants, we redesigned the nature of the supply chain by imparting local rules for all the underlying transportation.

Agent-based models are useful in problems in which we know (at least roughly) the local rules by which the agents behave. The unknown we want to discover is the emergent properties of the *collection* of agents.

Forecasting

Often the solution to a large class of problems is to generate a forecast: a future state of a system. Notice that I did not use the term "prediction"—a word I warned you about in chapter 1. The term "forecast" is a far better characterization, as it implies a calculated estimate of behavior as opposed to a highly accurate guess of the future state.

The structure in most all forecasting models consists of a series of data transformations until you get to the calculated future state. They could be as simple as a linear fit through a time series of data points, or as complex as a weather model that takes into account a large amount of real-time information on temperatures, pressures, and other atmospheric conditions. Forecasts occupy a special place in an organization's portfolio of analytics tools. More often than not, leaders will base decisions directly off of forecasts, giving them more gravity than other analytics exhibits. That in turn implies a degree of more care and handling than might be applied generally.

Bad forecasting

Most forecasting as it is done today in organizations is a complete waste of time. Worse yet, in some cases it is even misleading. I've seen more sins committed under the banner of forecasting than any other body of analytics. Why is this?

Forecasting is the "PowerPoint" of analytics—almost anyone can do it, but that does not mean it is done well. Planners often get caught up in "tool mode." Using some Excel add-in that actually generates numbers deludes them into thinking they have a reliable forecast.

Now to be fair, everyone at some point has to produce a forecast, and I don't fault people for trying their best. However, good forecasting practice, like good cooking, requires some thoughtful deliberation before jumping in. There is an entire science devoted to forecasting that should be grasped and respected. This is not a sport for amateurs.

Here I will offer a few tips and issues worth considering. It is by no means a full treatise on forecasting, but might help you align your thinking with good health and hygiene in this area:

1. **Bottom-up forecasts are almost always better than top-down**. Example: If you were forecasting an election, it would be better to do a forecast block by block and add it all up than do a county-wide aggregate.

2. **Transparency and process count for a great deal**. Before you even begin to write one line of code or enter data in a single cell, map out the progression of the forecast from raw data to final conclusion, most often with a picture. That will allow you to critique, refine, and explain the forecast to others.

3. **Absolute accuracy is far less important than getting more accurate over time**. Too many people focus on accuracy within a single cycle. However, that kind of thing comes and goes with the seasons. Rather, build a systemic way to true your results with actuals and measure the trend.

4. **Forecasting is all about distributions and not scalar numbers!** I can't tell you how many clients have sought to dumb down a good analysis by saying, "Just give me a single number." Resist this with everything you've got.

5. **What are you doing this for?** Many times, forecasts are seen as the solution to a problem. However, they may be a solution to a logic sequence, as in (1) "I need to know the weather tomorrow"; (2) "Why do you need to know the weather?"; (3) "Because I need to know if I need to bring my umbrella to work." In that case, having an umbrella at the office solves the same problem. Make sure these forecasts you are doing are essential to the *business problem* at hand.

6. **Speaking of distributions...** The tails of the distributions are where interesting things happen, like perfect storms of several conditions coming together to create an unlikely but very good or very bad event. Good forecasting practice suggests a careful examination of these outcomes *alongside* the ones near the mean.

7. **Forecasting is a daily, not a yearly sport.** Forecasts should be run and run again as fast as new data comes in. Only then will you get a feel for how the data steers the forecast.

8. **Excel can only take you so far.** I do not consider Excel to be the tool of choice for professionals. It is fine for small prototypes, but Excel's lack of separation of data from logic significantly reduces the transparency of the ultimate solution. For my money, I would much prefer a technical computing engine like *Mathematica*[1] on top of a database.

Forecasting is a deep science that should never be taken lightly. Consider the weight of all of the business decisions that may flow from your forecast—those decisions deserve more than a half-hearted effort by part-time resources.

Beyond the simplest forecasts, the logic is often constructed by subject matter experts throughout the organization. It is incumbent upon the analyst to carefully document the stepwise transformations into an overall design on paper to exist alongside the actual model. Special emphasis should be placed on the assumptions codified in the logic, including the naming of sources. Transparency is the cornerstone of best practice in forecasting.

Machine Learning

As of this writing, *machine learning* has become one of the hottest topics in data science. Although as a theoretical methodology it has been around for decades, it has in recent years become accessible to ordinary practitioners.

As the name implies, machine learning is the act of teaching a piece of software the relationship between a set of inputs and a set of outputs. Once taught, the model can then predict an output based on a set of inputs.

Let's say you wanted to predict how a particular person would vote in an election between two candidates, Joe and Sally. And let's say your theory is that such a prediction could be made by knowing a person's occupation, income, number of children, and the car they drive. You stand on a street corner, get the information, and construct a table of data. The structure is shown in Table 2.1.

Table 2.1 Survey of voters

Consultant	100K income	2 kids	Ford Fusion	Joe
Firefighter	50K income	3 kids	Jeep	Sally
Photographer	75K income	1 kid	Volvo	Sally
Journalist	80K income	None	Acura TSX	Joe
Receptionist	45K income	2 kids	Mini Cooper	Joe

The table itself is several hundred rows in length. The data is run through a machine-learning model.

It's the day after your data collection exercise, and you have your model in hand. You stop a person at random, and they give you the following information about themselves:

Sales, 110K income, 1 kid, Hyundai Sonata

When you submit that to your machine-learning model, it generates the following output:

Joe, 64.3 %, Sally, 35.7 % The model has indicated that the salesperson is more likely to vote for Joe, *based upon the way it was trained.*

The promise of machine learning lies in its ability to find correlations between data elements, while the challenge is to ensure that the model is trained properly. Therefore, machine learning, in spite of its moniker, is both art and science, with a critically important human judgment role.

Machine-learning models are superior for applications in which you have a wealth of data about a system, but need to make forward-looking forecasts and assertions about the system based on that data. The next time you hear, "Gee, we have lots and lots of data, but we don't know what to do with it," consider that a possible signal for the application of machine learning.

Key Point: Why "garbage in/garbage out" is…garbage

Some people might use "rule of thumb" to mean that input data has to be *perfect* in order for a model to be useful. Nothing could be further from the truth. Data that goes into models is *never* perfect, and in some cases is significantly flawed. The garbage comment misses the point—what is far more important is that your data and your assumptions are subject to sound health and hygiene. For example you should ask yourself the following questions:

1. Are the assumptions in the model clearly noted and do they have their sources listed?
2. Have you done a sensitivity check to see which data points have a stronger bearing on the outcome than others?
3. Have you used the filter in #2 to place special attention on the data points that more strongly drive the outcome versus less attention on those that do not?

These are just a few of the considerations of data health and hygiene that we will expand upon in chapter 3.

Monte Carlo Simulation

You will often be confronted with uncertainty in the business problems you face. Inputs to your models will not be known precisely; rather, a range of input values is likely. In these cases it will be handy to make use of a method known as the Monte Carlo simulation.

Let's say you were hired by a local developer to assess the financial prospects of a new 60-unit apartment complex to be built. Modeled very simply, the equation for annual revenue would be

Annual Revenue = Number of renters * monthly rent * 12.

The developer wants to lease the apartments at $1,200 per month. How many renters should we account for?

In my own observation, most people when confronted with uncertainty in the variables that make up their models will run several cases—three is the most common number, representing high, medium, or low expectations. Let's say in this situation, 30 rentals is the low case, 45 is the medium case, and all 60 units rented is the high case. This will generate revenue values of $432,000, $648,000, and $864,000 respectively. Human nature is predictable here. When presented with low/medium/high choices, everyone always focuses their attention on the middle ground; therefore, that $648,000 revenue number will take on outsize importance and will likely stick in the project team's mind. The other two numbers are forgotten.

To focus on the middle ground masks some very important subtleties in the output. The more likely case is the medium case, with high and low being less likely. But by how much?

Let's now say that you've commissioned a market research firm to find out the likelihood of the number of renters attracted to your apartment complex. They come back to you with a table, as shown in Table 2.2.

So, for example, there is an 84 percent chance that the number of renters in your apartments will *exceed* 40. A 2D plot of the table is shown in Figure 2.8.

This is also referred to as a cumulative distribution chart. Think of it as an odds chart showing the outcome of the number of renters, with the number being *very likely* in the 40 to 50 range, and much less likely on either side of the range.

Table 2.2 Survey estimate of the number of renters

No. of renters	% Chance no. of renters greater than the number at left
5	99%
10	99%
15	99%
20	99%
25	99%
30	99%
35	97%
40	84%
45	50%
50	15%
55	2%
60	0%

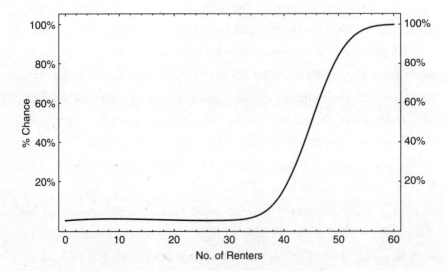

Figure 2.8 Cumulative probability of the number of renters

Let us "roll the dice" on a few plausible futures for our apartment complex, while weighting the dice in exactly the same way the chart above indicates. In 20 dice rolls, you might come up with the following outcomes:

{44, 36, 50, 51, 45, 50, 38, 51, 46, 51, 51, 45, 32, 48, 47, 47, 42, 40, 40, 55}

Notice that "most" of the outcomes were between 40 and 50, but on rare occasions they did extend outside of this range in the low end.

This is precisely what the Monte Carlo simulation does—it chooses random values, hundreds or thousands of times, and then produces a probability distribution of the outcome. Returning to our revenue formula above, we can now use the Monte Carlo simulation to model revenue.

The first random value in our list was 44. If there are 44 renters, the revenue is 44 * 1200 * 12 = $633,600. The second value is 36. If there are 36 renters, the revenue is 36 * 1200 * 12 = $518,400, and so on. If we ask our model to generate 100,000 dice rolls and calculate the revenue for each, we could generate a histogram of values, as shown in Figure 2.9.

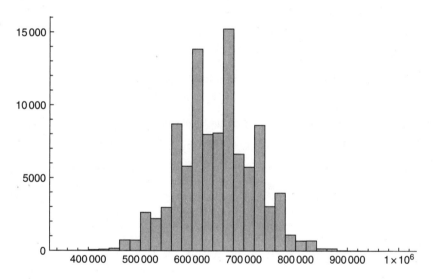

Figure 2.9   Probability distribution of revenue

Each bar represents a count of the revenues that fit within that band for the 100,000 tries. We are now in a much better position to advise our developer. Not only can we talk about the most likely revenue (around $650,000), but we can also speak more clearly about the extremes on either end of that mean. If the developer further reveals the costs of the apartment complex, we can now express the percentage likelihood of break-even.

The Monte Carlo simulation is ideal for those business problems that have a great deal of uncertainty around the key variables, and even more useful as the uncertainty begins to narrow over time as you acquire more information about the variables.

Key Point: The customer isn't always right

Models are complex beings. They don't always generate a single number, even for the same output metric. Sometimes the output is expressed as a range fitted along a probability distribution, as in the Monte Carlo simulation discussed above. Sometimes the output is a basket of measures expressing the performance of the model, in the same way that a student's report card shows grades across a list of subjects.

Often leaders in organizations, pressed for time and attention, will say to analysts, "I don't want to hear the explanation or ranges, just give me a number." It takes a great deal of fortitude to resist the temptation to comply, but resist you must. Dumbing down a complex solution from an even more complex problem will *inevitably enable poor decisions*. Rather, suggest to that executive that you will provide a story—a nicely structured narrative around the model outcomes that can be told in the space of a few minutes. It might be a graphic with very few words—something that will fit nicely on a slide if that's the chosen format—with plenty of annotations and sideline notes for coaching.

Data Envelopment Analysis

Imagine two car salespeople, Jim and Mary. Jim sells a beat-up Chevy van for $5,000. Mary sells a brand new Cadillac Escalade for $65,000. Which salesperson performed better?

Most organizations opt for simplistic measures of performance— either for assets or for humans. In sales organizations, it is most often the top-line revenue figure, or perhaps the contribution margin. In our example above, Mary would likely receive a congratulatory comment from the sales manager, while Jim would barely get noticed. But the question remains... who *performed* better?

The answer is not immediately clear. Jim may have done a bang-up job getting $5,000 for the Chevy—well above the market price—while Mary simply sold the Escalade at the average prevailing market price. Looking at it this way, Jim could have outperformed Mary *by doing more with what he was given*. This conundrum could be solved systematically by using a technique known as data envelopment analysis, or DEA.

DEA examines the activity of a producer, or decision-making unit (DMU)—any entity that can produce an output, given an input or set of inputs. Sales professionals are given a set of products and a territory (inputs), and are expected to produce sales (outputs) from that. For a whole collection of sales professionals, how can we make a fair comparison of their performance? Rating and ranking, like DMUs, from historical data is what data envelopment analysis does.

Let us walk through how DEA works using an example. Let's say we are looking at sales performance data from our car sales team over several months. There are two products sold: cars and trucks. How did each of the sales professionals do?

Our sales associate pool is diverse. Some of them are better at selling cars. They sell lots of them, but very few trucks. Others are truck people. They sell mostly trucks, but on occasion they also sell a car or two here and there. Let's plot their performance on a graph in which we measure just two performance metrics—truck sales and car sales (Figure 2.10).

Now let us draw a line (an envelope) around the outer perimeter of the best associates' scores. What emerges is an efficiency frontier representing the best possible performance of the group—the truck people and the car people, and everyone in between.

Finally, we take the performance of a randomly drawn associate. That person's "efficiency" is the proportion of the distance from the origin

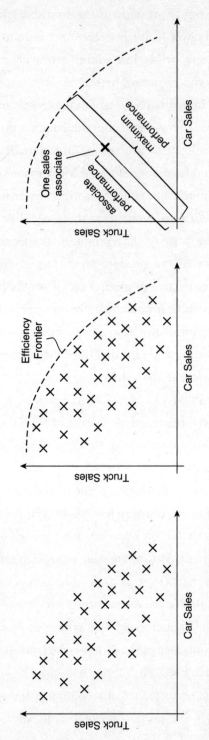

Figure 2.10 Data envelopment analysis example

at (0,0) to their position, and the distance from the origin to the efficient frontier at the same angle.

Where DEA comes in particularly handy is when there aren't just two measures of performance but several dozen. Or there are different territories, dealerships, and brands involved. DEA effectively equilibrates all of these differences and generates an efficiency score for all producers. It is important to note that the score is not carried against some arbitrary standard of performance, but rather is *self-referential*. The producer's performance is always on a scale against other producers, even as new producers come into view. If an especially good sales associate comes into the picture and outperforms all of the previous associates, that person's performance will move the efficiency frontier outward and lower all of the other associates' efficiencies, as it should do.

DEA is ideal for the problem of statistically fair rating and ranking of producers, be they salespeople, store branches, sports teams, machines, or operating assets. Moreover, DEA's self-referential nature allows the rating process to adapt to changes in the environment and in the producer population.

Heuristics

In my job as an analyst, I get a chance to share models I've built with a number of people. They will often say to me, "Wow, that model must have a lot of sophisticated math under the hood." Sometimes the answer is yes, but surprisingly, many of the models I have created involve no more than a handful of simple rules applied over and over. These rules are called heuristics, and they are the unsung heroes of analytics— not always recognized, but a very powerful means to solve crazy hard problems.

One of the classic mathematical examples of a very hard problem is that of routing, often referred to as the traveling salesman problem, or TSP. The setup is this: a salesman must visit N randomly scattered cities exactly once and return to a starting point (a tour). The problem is to find the exact sequence of cities that minimizes overall travel distance. What could be hard about that?

Here's what…a list of just 12 cities represents almost *500 million* possible routes!

But at first glance, it doesn't seem that hard. I could pull out a piece of paper and draw a reasonable route and probably get pretty close to the most efficient tour. The reason I can do that is that my brain is performing lots of heuristics—effectively throwing out many of the unreasonable tours in which the poor salesman is dashing hither and yon across the territory from one end to the other. My mental image is that of a reasonable order and distribution of stops, and I draw that on the paper.

Now if we can get a computer to do that, we can unleash it on any kind of routing, even randomly jostling the cities around and rerunning our model to accommodate.

Let's take a look at how we might devise a computer model to implement a heuristic for a routing problem. We've said that a heuristic is a simple rule, applied over and over. How about this one: from the starting point, find the nearest next point and make that the next stop. From that point, find its nearest next (unvisited) point and make that the next stop, and so on. We will call this the nearest neighbor rule, and our hope is that the heuristic will generate the best routing from start to stop, or at least a "good enough" route path. Using this rule and just a few lines of computer code, we would come up with a solution that looks like Figure 2.11.

It would be straightforward, then, to calculate the total distance traveled with this solution, which serves as a proxy of our solution's quality. Not bad, and probably very close to the optimal solution, which alternatively could be worked out with a lot of sophisticated computer code running for hours or days. If we achieve, say, 95 percent of the optimal solution with the heuristic, this may in fact be more preferable than spending lots of computer time eking out that last 5 percent. In my own experience with companies, I have seen many cases in which the good solution *now* is better than the perfect solution later (even an hour later).

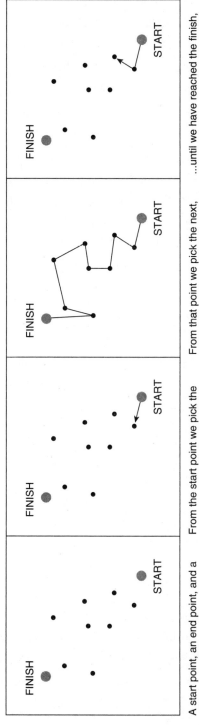

A start point, an end point, and a
number of stops in between

From the start point we pick the
nearest unvisited neighbor

From that point we pick the next,
and so on....

...until we have reached the finish,
giving us the heuristic's solution

Figure 2.11 Applying a heuristic to an example route from start to stop

Some heuristics build on other heuristics. So, for example, we could have another heuristic that takes the nearest neighbor outcome and does pairwise swapping of cities in the sequence, looking to improve (reduce) the total distance traveled. Or, we could have another heuristic that chooses a random first stop rather than the nearest first stop and so on. The beauty of heuristics is that they can be easily assembled, tested, and thrown away.

Heuristics are quite handy when you want a good solution fast versus a perfect solution in hours or days. Routing is a common application of heuristics, but so are business process design, scheduling/sequencing, and portfolio optimization.

Process/Flow Modeling

We live in a world of processes, most of which we don't even think about. Every time we buy that item in a store, there was an elaborate process that got it there. When we check out at the point-of-sale terminal we kick off a sophisticated financial transaction process among ourself, the store, our bank, and the store's bank. Business processes, as defined as chains of interrelated, specific tasks with a goal, are everywhere, which is why many industries are deeply concerned about how they work. A sample insurance process is shown in Figure 2.12.

It makes a great deal of sense to model processes and the flows of individual work items across them, because a model is a practical means for illustrating the performance of processes (throughput, cost, volume) under a wide variety of conditions.

Process modeling starts with a map, similar to the figure above, which elaborates all possible process steps and their input/output relationships to each other. With map in hand, we move to two fundamental concepts underlying the model: workflow tokens and flow of control. A token is created for each item, and the flow of control is the location of the token in the sequence of processes. For example, in our insurance claim example, a "token" is created representing our accident, and that token then flows,

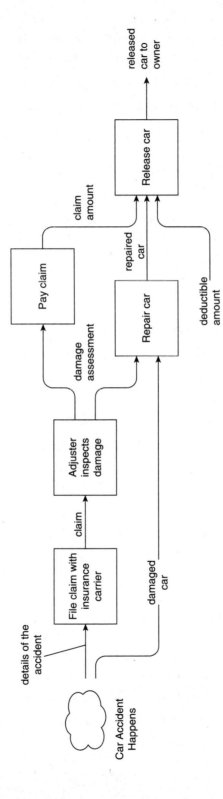

Figure 2.12 Process flow example

generally speaking, left to right across the page over time as our claim moves from one process step to another. The flow of control is the position of the token at any given instant. It is not uncommon for tokens to spawn other tokens, as in a testing process that generates a test result that flows through a very different set of process steps than the physical thing being tested.

The final ingredient in our process flow model is the rules by which each of the process steps operate—how does the process step transform the input into the output, and how long does that take? What kinds of resources are needed to perform the transformation, and what controls influence how it happens? The answers to these questions comprise the logic that is encoded into each process, which is the centerpiece of the simulation model.

The model can now be run by imparting workflow into the beginning step and allowing the processes to take that workflow forward to its natural conclusion over a simulated period of time. In many cases, analysts will use process flow models to stress test a particular workflow design against a wide variety of conditions—a process failure, very high volumes, or varying configurations of resources. An organization looking to design a new call center, for example, might build a process flow model with an array of different volume demands to see how the whole system behaves across varying conditions.

Process flow models are well suited for any problem that involves a sequence of steps, where the performance of that sequence is the question to be answered.

Chapter Summary

The prevailing theme of this chapter is that problem solvers must carefully match the attributes of the problem to the method or methods used to solve the problem. Successful matching is done through experience and judgment, but Table 2.3 is a useful starting guideline for those unfamiliar with a broad range of methods.

Table 2.3   Guidelines for matching problem to method

Problem features	Candidate methods
Uncertainty of system capacity or throughput Response to changes in resources Presence of physical or logical workflow	Process flow modeling

There are a vast number of excellent mathematical methods available for problem solving, and, surprisingly, more are being created every day. At this stage, you are now armed with the skill to recognize a problem and its features, and can move on to select a set of methods that are tuned precisely to those features. This is not a trivial skill, and will suit you well in a world filled with complex problems of every shape and size.

A durable process for solving a wide range of problems...check.

Methods to use within the process aligned with the problem type... check.

It is now time to talk about data.

CHAPTER 3

Data

A marine biologist straps a GPS tracking device to a sea turtle and releases it into the ocean. A friend of mine carries a pedometer on his wrist to record every step he takes throughout the day. Stand in line for a ride at Disney on any given day, and you will likely be handed a small slip of paper and told to hand it in at the head of the line.

We perform some strange gymnastics at times in our drive to collect *data*. Why?

Data is the "fuel" for any scientific investigation. Without it, we are left with guesswork. It is the alpha and the omega of serious problem solving, and deserves special attention, extra effort on data preparation and cleanup, and focus. In this chapter we will explore the salient aspects of data and how to successfully integrate it with the process and methods we have covered in previous chapters.

The primary form of data for use in business analytics is a set of measurements, for example, the sum of items delivered to point X on Y date from distribution center Z. This can be combined with all of the deliveries from all of the distribution centers across a range of dates to form a table of shipments. This data set then in turn could be used to analyze the performance of the supply chain. A sample of this kind of data is shown in Table 3.1.

Table 3.1   A sample of traditional business data

Item	Description	Destination	Origin	ShipmentID	Shipped
CKJ817	Rotary drill	OKC	Plant35	PNS338	4/14/2014
ISI214	Drum H2S	LROCK	Plant10	MHL184	4/20/2014
EWB627	Mount fixture	PITT	Plant35	TFQ516	4/17/2014
PTQ871	Controller	DEN	Plant16	FTY235	4/22/2014
PUZ824	Power supply	ORLO	Plant12	TAN219	4/27/2014
TXT226	Bracket	OMHA	Plant10	VKH828	4/15/2014
WGY886	Breaker assy	STLO	Plant19	ZDV919	4/18/2014

Measurement like this used to be expensive, difficult, and fraught with error, and served as the reason we could not help prevent sea turtles from becoming extinct or improve our health with important analytics. Today, however, measurement (as well as data storage) is nearly invisible, reliable, and practically free. *In a world in which measurement is free, data is boundless.* Therefore, we have a natural tailwind behind our problem-solving efforts that we did not have as recently as a half decade ago. This isn't simply good news, but it is also tremendously empowering.

What Is Data (and What Is Not)?

Even with sophisticated and elaborate equipment to capture information, it is important to realize which data is useful and, more importantly, which is not. A distinction should be made between parametric data— lists of customer addresses, race times for runners, a table of products in inventory—and information that speaks to the *logic* of a system, like the business rules that govern it. I make this distinction for two important reasons. First, some people refer to logic rules as data because it is acquired from subject matter experts in the same way that parametric data is acquired. However, that doesn't make it data. Logic tends to be static in nature, changing far less frequently than data. The rule by which you decide to take an umbrella with you to work changes less frequently than the daily chance of rain in your city. Logic and rules tend to become code in models, while data stays as data in tables in a database. The algorithm of pricing a product, the steps in forecasting demand, and the policies for the allocation of product shipments to delivery routes are all examples of logic and rules.

The second reason to make a distinction is to highlight the inherent problem of spreadsheets. Spreadsheets are excellent for storing raw data (numbers and text), but extending spreadsheet software into a complete model creates a lack of distinction between a formula (logic) in a cell and data (number or string). It is very difficult to unbind logic from data in a spreadsheet, and that makes spreadsheets unsuitable for anything other than very small problems. The larger the spreadsheet, the more convoluted the relationship between calculations and raw data. The story is lost. The bottom line: spreadsheets are very handy for *housing* raw data, but you should not try to make the spreadsheet a complete, stand-alone model except in all but the simplest of cases.

As of this writing, the very nature of data is changing. Our traditional view of data is strings and numbers, which are part and parcel of nearly everyone's mental model of the word "data." But what about images, objects, sounds, video clips, instructions, files, code, and web pages? All of these are data, just more complex structures than we often think of. Here is the good news: most modern data-managing systems, like database software, are quite capable of handling complex data, and you can see evidence of this all around you. Pull up an online catalogue listing from a retailer, and what do you see? An item is usually accompanied by a description and a price, perhaps a quantity on hand. But wait, there's more! Often included are images of the item, How-To videos, panoramic views, and downloadable apps. All of these things are kept in databases, and can be recalled at the whim of the user and pulled together into one comprehensive portrayal. So in your own work, don't forget about complex data in your taxonomy of information, which includes important *meta-data*—the "data about the data" that accompanies the core information.

Acquiring Data

To put data to good use, you must first get at it. That sounds rather trivial, but in my experience acquiring data can be one of the most labor-intensive parts of the problem-solving process—a counterintuitive notion, maybe, but true.

We start with which data is needed to solve our problem. Here again is where lots of organizations get it wrong—they pursue a vigorous and time-consuming data collection exercise *before* defining the analytical model at hand. They do this because, either they don't know what else to do, or they worry that the data that is needed won't be available. The result is a lot of wasted effort collecting the wrong data or a failure to collect the right data, or, worse, they might conclude, "why bother to build a model?" if the data is missing or of low quality.

The best way to identify the data needed by the model is to consult the qualitative model. This blueprint should clearly spell out the data needed as it shows just what variables are included in the "calculus" of the problem. For example, the qualitative model might call out a variable called *Vendor*, which is used to establish a profile of a participant in your supply chain. That implies a table of sorts in your data to house all of the salient information about all vendors in the system. In our own work, we often generate a *data model*—a graphical depiction of the data structure— directly from the qualitative model.

Now that you have an inventory of which data to acquire, set about the task of getting it. And here is where the good news comes in. Now, more than ever before, we have access to a wealth of information, much of it public and free. Want to know the female labor force participation rate in Pakistan? Consult the *World Bank Labor Data* catalogue. Wholesale electricity prices in the United States in 2009? That's the Energy Information Administration. The vote count for Place 4 in the Duncanville (Texas) Independent School District school board election in March 2014? Try Ballotpedia. The road network for the state of Pennsylvania? Go to the Stanford Large Network Dataset Collection.

Coming to America

I'm sitting in my office on a comfortable afternoon when I get a phone call. It is from a very excited gentleman who wants me to help him with some analysis. He explains that he has heard of a "special" source of data that will really help his business. He wants to see me... *now*.

Reluctantly, I agree to meet him. He explains that he is in the industrial materials business, and his crosstown rival is ruining his margins and stealing market share. He wants to analyze the competitor's operations to find out what they are up to.

"Sir, I understand your plight, but as your competitor is a privately held company, there is very little data I could get on them that would be useful." He leans forward and in a low, raspy voice says, "*but you can see what they import.*" It turns out that he had read an article about amateur corporate sleuths getting goods import data from the US Customs and Border Protection to predict everything from new product launches to shortages leading to price increases. I had real doubts about the existence of such data, but I agreed to do some research.

It turns out that the man was exactly right.

It is now possible to get information on all items shipped into the United States from other countries—down to the particular container on a particular ocean liner showing up at a particular port on a particular day. Astonishing. From this data I was able to extract the competitor's import information and highlight on a timeline the shipments of raw materials, sliced by country of origin and commodity type.

The gentleman thanked me, paid his bill, and walked out of my office, never to be heard from again. I have no idea what he did with my analysis, but I hope he found what he was looking for.

Increasingly we are seeing third-party providers step forward as *aggregators* of data—organizations that take disparate sets of data and compile it (for a fee) in a more friendly, consistent, and organized format than the source data exists on its own. One example of many is Platt's, a unit of McGraw Hill Financial, which provides market data for energy-related commodities from coal to petrochemicals, using a wide variety of sources from various governments and clearinghouses.

Reenactment

There is quite the cottage industry of war re-enactors. I had the chance to witness an American Civil War re-enactment, and it was something to see. The participants donned very detailed uniforms and period weaponry. Precise maps of certain charges were carried out in accordance with a very authentic timeline. The experience was as emotional as it was fascinating. This group of people rewound time by 150 years, giving us a highly accurate glimpse of a nation-shaping event.

A week or so after that experience, I found myself sitting in a conference room as a participant in an after-action process at an oil company. It seems that a particular drilling operation had gone badly wrong, was eventually corrected, and now the team was assembled to openly discuss what went wrong and how to prevent such failures in the future. I applaud the company for doing this—most firms move on from failures for political reasons—looks-backs are rare.

Yet the process used for this oil company was decidedly qualitative. The attendees argued back and forth over a dizzying array of technical data for a while, settled on a few root causes, assigned one of the team to write up a summary memo, and adjourned the meeting.

What if, instead, we could re-enact the failed operation in the same way the amateur historians re-enacted the battle? In fact, could we go even further—could we stop the re-enactment at any time, put it in slow motion, rewind it, and add a few more soldiers here and there? Simulation makes this completely feasible.

I convinced the oil company team to simulate the drilling failure, minute by minute, as we had a wealth of measured data on what happened in the days leading up to the failure. All of this was layered upon a realistic, visual model of the drilling operation that we could watch over and over. The team spotted not one but several contributing factors lining up just so, to create a "perfect storm" scenario that ultimately led to the failure. The model was archived in the company's systems so that any team could use its findings. Re-enactment, in simulation terms, is one of the most powerful ways in which companies can exploit the power of institutional learning.

Governments are getting into the act as data providers. Transport For London (TfL), which operates the famous London Underground, makes the position of every active train available for free on its web service, which is updated every 30 seconds. Data.gov, in the United States, is a massive open data archival effort of everything from education to banking. Similar efforts are going on in Canada, Denmark, and Australia.

Private data inside of organizations is undergoing a quieter but no less dramatic transformation. Beginning in the 1990s, businesses spent millions on implementing enterprise-wide information systems like SAP and Oracle, with the governing philosophy of having a "single version of the truth" record of business activity and financial reconciliation. While the motivation was more around streamlined and uniform operations globally, the end result was cleaner, broader, more useful data. Even smaller firms mirrored the trend, with appropriately sized business systems replacing disparate vertical applications that were not well integrated. In short, nearly every organization has stepped up its game in the last decade or two with respect to enterprise software, and problem solvers get a collateral benefit from that.

Humans are the most challenging of data sources. In every organization there are certain people who are deemed experts in particular areas. We call these people subject matter experts, or SMEs for short. Your job is to interview the SMEs and glean the salient data elements from them.

Data Amplification

Have you ever wondered why we run out of things? That special, hot, new toy at Christmas that is impossible to find; your favorite cereal that the grocery store sells out of; the daily special that the restaurant cannot make because they have run out of the main ingredient. Are we not modern and sophisticated enough with our supply chains to avoid these seemingly frequent stockouts?

What you are experiencing is the consequence of the problem of *data amplification*, a situation that you as a problem solver must understand well. Why do establishments run out? As with any business, they measure the things that are easy to measure, and inventory on hand fits that category well. So a good business person, seeking to reduce working capital costs, tries to keep inventories of items on hand as lean as possible. What is not measured is the response from the disappointed customer who really, really wanted that item. When was the last time you saw the person from the store write down your displeasure at not having an item? It never happens. So when making an important decision about inventory, the business-person is only clearly seeing one side of the problem—the working capital side. Therefore, more often than not the decision is tilted that way, and customers bear the brunt.

The key learning point for the problem solver is to be alert to the data amplification problem and seek to create a balance in your measurement efforts so that decisions aren't artificially swayed by the easily measurable variables.

SMEs spend their whole careers involved in the details of what they do, and therefore believe that *every little detail* is extremely important. Remember Occam's Razor from chapter 1? Every detail is *not* equally important, and it is up to you to distinguish the relevant from the immaterial. You will make these delineations using personal judgment and the hypothesis.

You may not realize it, but you actually practice deriving data from SMEs every time you read the newspaper. There are lots of words in the article, but your brain is distilling them down into the key significant points. When interviewing SMEs, you should have a clear line of questioning in mind, and not worry about interrupting them in midthought if necessary. Working with SMEs is all about peeling back layers, understanding the concept, validating what you think you know, then peeling back some more. Your goal is to gather "how the system works" by taking a joint tour with the SME through day-in-the-life vignettes of how things get done by the system that sits at the center of the problem at hand—the logic and rules that underpin that system. The qualitative model that you are building piece by piece becomes your journal of those conversations.

On the nonhuman side, the latest revolution in data acquisition comes from the emergence of small, highly intelligent computers with an array of sensors sitting inside of mundane devices. Smart energy meters in your home, devices you attach to your car to lower insurance rates, wearable computers that measure your activity level throughout the day—these are common consumer examples. Organizations are beginning to apply the same ideas with small, general-purpose computers no bigger than a credit card that are attached to equipment, people, buildings, and products. The revolution is called the *Internet of Things*, in which each of these devices has its own unique presence on the Internet, streaming data from its sensors at real-time speeds.

All of this progress has brought leading thinkers into the data space to talk about the concept of total recall—near perfect and complete recollection of historical events, good and bad. Minute-by-minute streams of data are continuously recorded and replayed up to some big event. It is the closest experience we have to reverse time travel, and the practice can reveal some amazing insights into cause-and-effect relationships living inside of complex systems.

Crowdselling

Valuable data can pass through our hands invisibly. Such was the case for a pharmaceutical firm. Every business day, sales representatives would fan out in cities all over the world to work with physicians, clinics, and hospitals on the range of medications the company had in its portfolio. Thousands of interactions between the rep and customers occurred every minute. At the end of the day, reps were asked to fill out an electronic journal on their mobile phones or tablets (they prefer not to lug around laptops) as to how the day's discussions went.

I asked the company whether they systematically mined the data in these journals. "It's too hard," one information technology (IT) director told me. "Everyone writes in their own style, and even uses different codes and words to describe the same thing, so it's hard to extract the meaning from their text notes in a useful way." So the most valuable data for this company—the "last mile" interactions between the company and its customers—is wasted. What a shame. There had to be another way.

After some thought, we came up with an idea: what if analytical models existed as nodes on private company social networks? Reps could "tweet" summaries of their interactions as the day unfolded. Models could read the postings, analyze their content, and tweet back trends and other global statistics that reps could in turn use for subsequent customer meetings. It is as if each rep could harness the power and intelligence of the entire sales force in real time. Here's how it works, using mythical sales rep Jill to tell the story:

Jill is in Dr. Smith's office to speak about a new asthma treatment that was just released by her company. The meeting goes well, and Jill tweets a quick report:

Jill: *"Just had a great visit with an ENT who said Sybprofen will fit nicely, especially for patients 18 YO and less."*

It turns out that this uptrend in favorability to the new asthma treatment is especially strong in the Southeast—after some checking, it appears that this is due to a load of new cases (as reported by the Centers for Disease Control) as well as a couple of recent research reports from Europe.

The model responds by highlighting these points back out to the network

Model: *"Sybprofen is trending higher in acceptability in younger patients in Southeast US. Click here for research reports and success messages from the field."*

Sales reps around the globe see these messages, adapt their pitch, and interact with customers, generating their own results and sharing messages.

Don't overlook valuable data that is currently invisible. It could lead to substantial transformations in capability and performance.

No matter how the data comes to you, it is important to organize it in a way that allows anyone to step into your world of data and understand it very quickly. Here are a few tips:

- Use clear, simple folder names and hierarchies to store raw files like spreadsheets, images, or text files.
- Use the "properties" feature of electronic files to note sources, content description, and dates.
- Applications like Evernote can be very handy as they use a tagging feature to apply markers to files and notes. Information in Evernote can then be searched by tag.

If you have a live data source for a computer model, such as a database that is directly connected to it, work out a well understood scheme for who is allowed to change the data, a clear process for making the changes, and a version control system for rolling back changes as needed.

Granularity

Here is a key principle to remember: Granularity = Realism. The more granular our data, the closer we get to an approximation of the real system's behavior. Taking a snapshot of an intersection every 30 seconds is less realistic than capturing a video of that intersection at 30 frames per second. As a problem solver, you will frequently be called to make judgments about what level of realism, and therefore what level of granularity, is "just good enough" to satisfy the hypothesis question, but stops short of adding unnecessary effort.

Think of your favorite weather app. When you want to find out what the weather will be near your home, the app asks you to enter the zip code or postcode of your residence. You would find it annoying if it asked you to type in the complete address before handing you the latest forecast, because your expectation is that the weather doesn't change that much across a postcode, and an approximation like that will do just fine. If weather models were precise enough to pinpoint the weather right above your house, would that be nice to have? Sure it would, but the time and energy it would require for you to type in the full address is clearly not worth the effort. So the granularity of the weather app at a postcode level is the "just right" trade-off between effort versus accuracy.

The same considerations should be taken into account when thinking about the granularity of data. Most often there is an inflection point in the spectrum of data collection, at which the effort expended to get those last few sets of details is very high, with limited benefits. As mentioned previously, the hypothesis is an excellent guide for making decisions about data granularity. The key is to match the granularity of the data with the granularity of the decision to be made from the analysis.

Data Privacy and Security

There will be times when the data that you work with in problem solving will be sensitive at some level. Companies are understandably reluctant to freely push data out of tightly controlled repositories into models, but push they must if the data is to be made useful.

The first step is to look at the nature of the data, examining which parts are sensitive and which are not. In my own experience I have found that the vast majority of data elements are not sensitive—a precious few are, but people tend to brand an entire table of data as "highly confidential" when that does not tell the full story.

Let me give you an example of how you can use a surgical approach to your advantage. Let's say you have a list of customers from a retailer shown in Table 3.2, and you want to analyze that data to show which customers most frequently shop at which stores.[1] As you can see, it includes customer name, address, some purchase history, affinity status, and a range of other fields comprising a profile of all customers. The retailer would be correct in thinking of this as very sensitive information— not only to be protected from potential competitors but also to protect customer identities from leaking beyond the boundaries of the retailer's internal systems.

The first step is to *de-identify* the data. Two elements of the table identify a customer down to an individual—the name and the address. However, if you are only interested in doing a frequency/location analysis, the customer name is irrelevant to you. Therefore, when we extract the information, we simply ask the retailer to strip these fields from the data. All we need is a customer ID of some sort. Table 3.3 shows a de-identified version of the customer list.

On occasion I have run into a situation in which several retailers share customer ID schemes, or possibly use public IDs (like Social Security numbers, birthdates or driver's license numbers) to generate the customer ID. In these cases, you could encrypt the ID using a simple key that the data owner, in this case the retailer, would retain exclusively. So, for example, a customer with an original ID of A2389698649 becomes derived ID Z6437384639 after encryption, and only the retailer can reverse the latter into the former using a software-based key. Another nice feature of

Table 3.2 An example of sensitive information: a customer table

Name	Address	City	St	ZipCode	Last Purchased Item	Affinity Program	Online
Jim Sarver	1025 Harvest Turnabout	Chester	PA	15017	ZLC329	Y	N
Abbey Fehr	9695 Pleasant Lake Mall	Windrose	AL	35051	ICW547	N	N
Rhea Fenn	353 Sunny Barn Terrace	Carterville	NE	68044	AEJ480	Y	Y
Jonathon Gundersen	8344 Dusty Mountain Rd	Jamestown	NC	27051	NVI237	Y	Y
Mary Jorden	8949 Fallen Boulevard	Juniper Valley	CA	90016	TQV709	N	Y
Amanda Zehner	9605 Velvet Glen	Raynesworth	GA	30036	POX822	N	N
Rory Plaster	1469 Broad Rabbit Street	Temple City	OK	73074	CCU280	Y	Y
Tara Coll	3396 Middle Beacon Parade	Amity	MS	38641	BLP851	N	Y
Ben Meyer	8888 Foggy Manor	Homestead	UT	84083	FPO944	N	N
Hilda Gilyard	8654 Stony Field	Icarus	VT	05362	CUS362	Y	N

Table 3.3 Customer table after de-identification

CustomerID	ZipCode	Last Purchased Item	Affinity Program	Online
SQN95368	15017	ZLC329	Y	N
MUB52869	35051	ICW547	N	N
GGT67545	68044	AEJ480	Y	Y
WAL54509	27051	NVI237	Y	Y
GDX13160	90016	TQV709	N	Y
LHT60031	30036	POX822	N	N
CDL37594	73074	CCU280	Y	Y
NDD71152	38641	BLP851	N	Y
RKR43567	84083	FPO944	N	N
HNN47177	05362	CUS362	Y	N

encryption is that it allows you to distinguish the same ID as it appears multiple times in a data set. "Hidden" customer Z6437384639 will always be customer Z6437384639 no matter how many times they appear in the data. Figure 3.1 shows how de-identification works relative to the data owner and the analyst.

It is important to note that de-identification goes beyond morphing the personally identifiable data, additionally ensuring that reasonable guesses from the data cannot be made. For example, if you've stripped the patient name from a record, yet still indicate that this person lives in a certain zip code and has a very rare condition, it is possible in theory to make a pretty good guess as to who that person might be. Or if you have a list of energy consumers in a town in which there is only one huge manufacturing plant, one might guess who the largest consumer might be. Good practice is to continue to de-identify until no reasonable guesses for uniquely identifying organizations or individuals can be made.

As addresses are dropped, you lose the customer's location. Doesn't that prevent us from doing the frequency/location analysis? It does negate street-level location, but preserving just the zip code or postcode out of the address still allows a viable, although slightly less precise, frequency/location analysis to be done (remember what we said about granularity

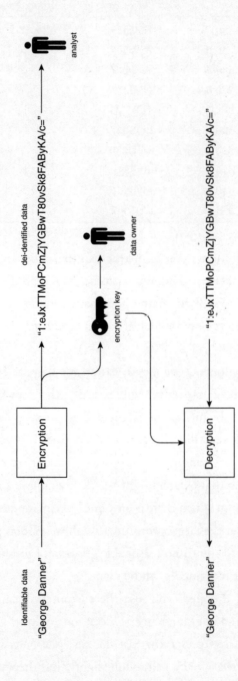

Figure 3.1 Data de-identification

earlier?). This is a process known as *data distillation*—stripping the unnecessary bits of data from the full set to derive just the minimal information needed to conduct the analysis.

Yet another effective method for dealing with sensitive data is *synthesis*, generating fake but realistic data from small samples or profiles of actual data. For example, if you have 100,000 customers, of whom 55,000 are female and 45,000 are male, each with an income range from $20,000 to $180,000, it is a fairly straightforward matter to manufacture 100,000 fake customers (or fake orders, or fake widgets) in data using statistical random draws that resemble the actual customer population.

All of these methods add up to a counterintuitive philosophy of data privacy—putting more of an emphasis on making the analysis data itself less sensitive rather than locking up the sensitive data behind iron walls.

Huge Data Sets

Whether it is due to the decreasing cost of storage, the emphasis on measurement, or the increased availability of public data, there is no question about it—our data is getting bigger. Consider this: you could store the entire text of the US Library of Congress on a set of hard drives that today would cost you about $1,800, or about 9 cents per gigabyte.

The term "big data" is all the rage in IT circles. In our practice, we've worked with a data set of every voting age adult in the United States (238 million people) and every building in the United Kingdom (28.5 million buildings), and multidimensional seismic data for the oil and gas industry in the tens of gigabytes in size.

There are several implications here for the average problem solver. Large data sets require more care and handling than a data set that is, say, on the order of a few hundred thousand records by a few dozens of fields. You may be accustomed to tossing some data onto a spreadsheet or a small local database. These larger data sets, however, must be housed in sophisticated relational database systems. This in turn requires that many of the tasks you once performed manually—lookups, updates, extracts—will now have to be accomplished with code.

For example, to copy an entire column of data in a spreadsheet is just a series of point-select-click actions. With very large data sets you would perform that same operation with Structured Query Language (SQL) statements. To look over some data to make sure it is correct in a spreadsheet, you simply scroll through it. Larger data sets require a piece of code to be written to "look," in an automated way, at the validity of the data.

When it comes to bringing large data into a model for analysis, it is important to recognize the scope of the data needed per unit of computation. Do I need to spin through every single customer out of 1.6 million in order to perform my analysis, or can I narrow it to particular kinds of customers, like only those with total purchases greater than $50? *Pareto filtering*, which focuses on a smaller but more influential subset of the data, not only cuts down on the computation time but also prevents the model from being skewed toward data with less of a bearing on your outcome.

Making Data Useful

Dealing with Bad and Missing Data

The problem of data availability and quality still lingers. In my own practice I have had promising, valuable problem-solving projects grind to a halt because some crucial piece of data could not be found. This issue is frustrating and inexcusable in these modern times.

Missing and bad data is part of every model ever produced. However, this is not an excuse to forgo modeling—in fact, this should never be a reason to defer a modeling project, because in such situations data quality will inevitably improve, and when it does, you will need a ready "home" for that data—the model. When Google Earth was released in 2005, not all of the satellite imagery for the whole of the planet was available. Major cities tended to be high resolution, while some outlying areas were grainy, low resolution. As the new satellite imagery became available, Google gradually improved the app, region by region. Today, almost all of the coverage is high resolution. The key point is that Google did not wait until all the data was in perfect order to release a very useful product, and you shouldn't either.

One substitute for bad or missing data is professional judgment and assumptions. That may surprise you, that is, that soft aspects like "judgment" are incorporated into quantitative models. But it is true— professional judgment and assumptions underlie almost every model ever built, and that is not a bad thing. What is important is making these assumptions *completely transparent*, and documenting the source of them carefully. In my own work, I consider the "assumptions list" document one of the most important artifacts of the model-building process.

Data Cleansing

Most raw data has to be straightened out and fixed before it can be made useful in analytics. The units could be off, for example, meters versus feet, or the set of codes for widgets could be slightly different from the codes for wadgets. Then there are downright errors, in which, say, a number that should *always* be positive shows up as negative in a few cases.

It is very common to use spreadsheets for data cleansing, as they can perform operations on data rows (and columns) selectively and easily. However, spreadsheets are not as effective when you have multiple tables that have to be cleansed at once and/or the data is very large.

In these cases, it is often handy to write small programs to act on the data to cleanse it. These same programs can also validate that the cleansing operation was conducted correctly, and support as well the population of the database system with the cleansed data. IT organizations often refer to these small programs as exchange, transact, and load, or ETL utilities.

Later, we will introduce you to a few software tools that are tailor made to the function of small programs that can act on data.

Normalizing Data

At the beginning of the chapter, we introduced the idea of a data model. As the name implies, it is a logical map of all of the entities or objects in the system, and the relationships among them. So if I have a table of Customers, as shown in Figure 3.1, in which each row in that table is a unique individual customer, this then relates to another table of Purchases, because customers make purchases, and for a particular customer, I can look up in the Purchases table all of the purchase rows that are associated with that table. The key that makes this happen is the customer ID. The useful information about each object is formed of fields listed below the banner in the table, shown in Figure 3.2.

Excellent books have been written on data design and management, and I do not intend to re-create that large body of work here. However, I will say that the creation of a logical map of your data, especially the data that the models will use directly in their calculations, is essential. I recommend the use of well-proven techniques for representing data, such as entity relationship diagramming (ERD), customizing it as needed. No matter the technique, our goal should be a one-to-one correspondence between the objects called out in the diagram and the

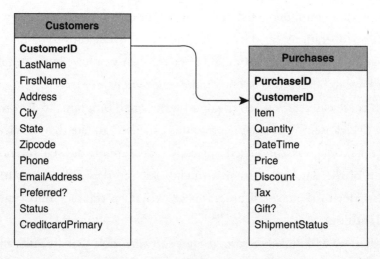

Figure 3.2 A customer table linked to a purchase history table

table structures that exist in the actual data source, a spreadsheet, or a database. This will make the transition from the data model on paper to the implementation of the data sitting in some software system much easier and less error prone.

Data Discovery

You've now done all the good health and hygiene to get your data in a good place—a well-organized library whose slices can easily be pulled into an analytical environment for calculations.

Now what?

If a simulation model is your goal, then that model's code can connect to your data source, suck in the salient data, and simulate the system at hand. However many situations aren't quite as straightforward. Perhaps you are simply responding to an executive's observation that "we have lots and lots of data, we just don't know what to do with it."

Raw data doesn't magically tell you what it knows—you have to tease out the patterns lying underneath the vast rows and columns before you. This process is known as *data pathology*, borrowing from the metaphor of human pathology, in which the body is cut open and examined, with no pretext as to what will be found there. The data analogue of a pathology uses tools and methods to slice, reorder, and perform computations on the data to force it to reveal its mysteries. The following are a few common data pathology methods that require relatively little sophistication.

Sorting

The simple act of sorting data can be very revealing, yet you would be surprised how often organizations overlook this very simple analysis frame. Who are in the top 10? The bottom 50? How much (revenue/units/volume) does the top 10 account for? Are the results Pareto distributed (relatively small population accounting for a relative large proportion of something)?

Fragmented sorting moves down the hierarchy to sort in blocks (best cricket players in England vs. the best cricket players from India). Horizontal sorting takes the same data set and selectively sorts by every sortable column in that set to see how the top or bottom lists change. Sorting is one of the easiest analytical steps you can do, so take advantage of that and sort in as many ways as available—you may be surprised what you find (and that is the point).

Graphing

The human brain cannot comprehend a data series longer than about four to six elements. In other words, the average person cannot *see* the trend of data in their mind for all but the very simplest of data sets.

One commonly overlooked perspective is the graph matrix—a series of graphs that tell a story both individually and in sequence, by using the same scaling for each cell. Figure 3.3 shows an example of production data for a network of factories. Notice how certain features are self-evident when illustrated this way:

- January started very slowly but dramatically ramped up—perhaps due to a shortage?
- March fell behind in the early part of the month, but then snapped back smartly at the end
- Total production month on month gradually increases from January to July, then just as gradually declines from July to December.

Distribution

What are the relative magnitudes of the numerical attributes of the population, one to another? They may consist of something like adult height, which is relatively uniform and for which there is a small number of exceptions. Plotting the height of every adult in your data set will likely reveal a flat-looking line. Or, they might include personal income, or the populations of cities in a country, which is power-law distributed

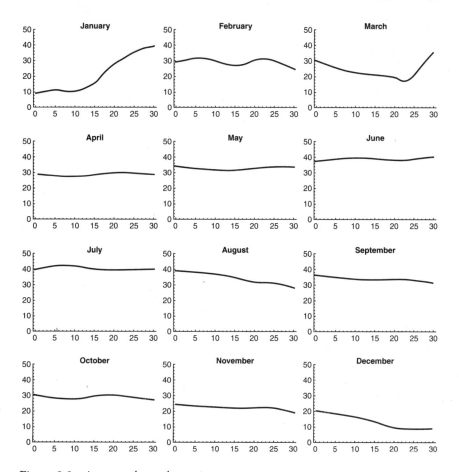

Figure 3.3 An example graph matrix

(a rank-ordered curve from largest to smallest curve shows an exponential decline). The "shape" of certain elements of data can speak volumes, and can confirm or refute widely held beliefs that are rarely tested. I've sat through many meetings with companies that say things like, "Our customers are all ___" or "We never see orders larger than ___." Many of these mental models turn out to be wrong, or perhaps too simple. A quick check of the distributions of data attributes can be very revealing.

Clustering

What data points are like other data points? Are there natural groupings to my data? Clustering applies statistical filters to data as a means of grouping it logically. Voters for a particular candidate, for example, might fit certain ranges around income, education, age, or home location.

The images in Figure 3.4 represent just such a perspective. On the left-hand side we see what appears to be random data (and it is). On the right-hand side we have applied a clustering algorithm to find the natural boundaries in the data—three groups were deduced and are marked as such.

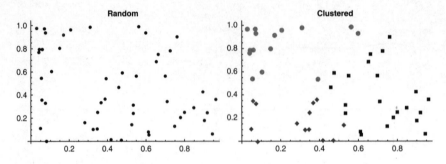

Figure 3.4   Clustering data

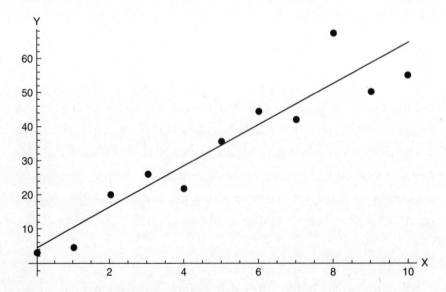

Figure 3.5   Linear regression example

Regression

A simple linear regression pits two variables against each other to determine their correlation. Does crime rate increase with temperature in summer months? How do sales change with the number of products?

Figure 3.5 shows a best-fit correlation between a variable X and another variable Y. Correlations can be strong and reliable, or weak and indeterminate as measured by the statistical indicator R squared, the coefficient of determination.

These are just a few of the methods that comprise rapid and effortless ways to uncover patterns in data even before a tangible hypothesis is formed.

The Next (Big) Data Thing: Data Curation

Having a lot of great data is one thing. Making widespread use of its insights across an organization is another. We have grappled with data usefulness for quite a long time, and until now our efforts have resulted in nothing more than the automation of dashboards and tabular reports. Yawn.

Try this simple test. Imagine a college student walking into your organization with no particular background in your industry. That college student wants to ask some simple questions about the organization. They might ask the following:

1. How many units of type__ did you sell a year ago?
2. When a customer orders a product, what is the process for delivering it?
3. Who is your main competitor and how are they doing financially?

The questions above would have to be tailored to your organization, of course. But anyone can imagine a set of simple questions a disassociated observer could ask.

How hard is it to generate an answer to these?

I've done this test myself with a few executives. The answer is astonishing. Instead of, "I have that at my fingertips," more often than not it is,

"Our IT team says it will take two weeks and a $100K budget to get that," and one quite embarrassed executive. Most leaders are stunned to find out how difficult and time consuming it is to get answers to the most basic questions, the ones that aren't preprogrammed into some dashboard or monthly report (and even those were ridiculously labor intensive to set up in the first place). For one reason or another, we have engineered extreme rigidity into our production IT systems, doing a handful of things exhaustively at the expense of doing a broad range of functions flexibly.

In recent years we have seen a possible solution to the college student problem called *data curation*. The term "curation" is similar to that of a museum curator, whose job is to carefully document and assess the objects coming into the museum, gathering *meta-data* on the objects so that they can later be retrieved, displayed, or researched. Notice that curation is an *active process*, not just storage. The same is true for data. When data is curated, one goes through a process of considerable rigor to establish its meaning and context. The data concepts of something simple like an aspirin tablet are the following: (1) it is a physical object with a size and weight; (2) it has a chemical makeup; (3) it is a pharmaceutical used in pain relief; (4) it is a consumer product, marketed under several brands, and so on. All of the aspects of the data object aspirin are compiled so that a computer can understand all of its meanings.

Once a large body of information is curated, we can return to the idea of asking sensible questions, like "What is the best aspirin to take with me on my vacation?"

Natural language-processing technology, while nascent, has progressed to a level of usefulness that we are beginning to see in our daily lives, in applications such as Siri on smartphones. It works by breaking down sentences such as the one above into instructions for the computer to process:

1. The user wants to know about aspirin, a pharmaceutical.
2. The word "best" implies a choice of aspirin (probably by brand), and it requires a rank ordering.

3. The user will be on vacation, which means away from home. The location of the vacation might be important in the ranking (dry climate? interactions with certain foods?)

The computer devises a strategy for answering the question by following logical threads through each part of the investigation above. Because both the private data about the user and public data on aspirin have been curated, this kind of query is predisposed to allowing a computer program to assemble the knowledge needed to traverse the user's question.

The computer moves through the data (list of aspirin brands available near the user's home, with recommendations from a medical website, past purchases of aspirin, other medications the user is taking) to follow a trail of deduction that ultimately leads to a list of aspirins, and their prices and availability at various retail stores within a five-mile radius of the user's home.

Now imagine that same power applied to an organization with vast amounts of internal data about its makeup and operations. Private curation enables sensible questions, expressed in natural language, to be answered in sensible ways. *This is the future of intelligence from data.*

Chapter Summary

Data is the oxygen of analytics—we cannot solve problems without it. Yet the care and handling of data is the most challenging aspect of problem solving. Not to worry. Follow a few key principles in acquiring data and making it useful to computer models, and you will be basking in data glory. Moreover, you will have established a regimen for the organization so that, as data continues to grow in volume and variety, you will be in a position to exploit its underlying patterns quickly.

Speaking of patterns, one way to make our data conjure up self-evident patterns is through *visualization*. We will take a look at how to create effective and compelling visualizations in the next chapter.

CHAPTER 4

The Art of Science: Visualization

Early in my career my boss came to me with a proposition: how would I like to present my most recent findings to the chief executive officer?

Wow. Yes. Of course! When??

Now was my chance to show how important my findings were to the company and how we could capitalize on their insight. I had my analysis, backed by reviews with my peers, and all the spreadsheets were in place.

About a week later, the day came for me to make my presentation. The CEO greeted me heartily at the door. After courtesies were exchanged, we got down to business. I launched into my findings, highlighting the progression of raw data to intermediate calculations to findings to conclusion—just like I had rehearsed dozens of times before in the week prior.

"Wait one minute," he said. "I'm not sure I follow the relationship between our units sold in the second quarter to our carrying costs up to that point."

I then pointed back to the screen. "Well, the data shown here in this cell is related to the data over there via this formula. Let me open up the cell so that you can see the formula I used." Silence.

One of his lieutenants spoke up. "Hmmm...that raises a question I had. Shouldn't the supply chain velocity calculation take into account the effect of back orders?" Now it was my turn to be silent.

A faceless executive from the back of the room said, "And where is your assumption for weighted average cost of capital. It's really important to get that right. If not, your model is pretty much useless."

I don't really remember much after that. All I remember is that at some point there were some muffled "thank yous" from the group as I staggered out of the room completely deflated.

What went wrong? I did everything right—I had a cogent story backed by data. My calculations were sophisticated and accurate.

Sound familiar? Everyone has their Waterloo story—the places and actors change, but the dreadful experience is about the same.

It took me nearly a decade to figure this out, but finally it hit me: It is simply insufficient to get the answer to a business problem, one *must be prepared to explain that answer to a wide variety of bright people who are nonetheless not analysts, mathematicians, or data scientists.* Even "telling a story" with data is not adequate—you have to put the story in motion in real terms to the audience in front of you. And you have to do all of that in a nonmathematical way.

The solution is, of course, visualization.

My spreadsheets did not allow the CEO to "see" the relationships that he wanted to understand. I was talking him through my answer, when he wanted to be taken on a "day in the life" journey through the real system and how it worked, and how it might work differently with the changes I was proposing. That CEO is not alone—most of the leadership you will deal with has the same kind of disposition to complex business problems, which is why you need to master visualization if you are to have any hope of success in problem-solving.

I made the classic mistake of assuming my analysis alone would carry the day, and did not consider the important role visualization plays in allowing our models to self-explain the systems we analyze. These days I see many others making the same mistake.

In this chapter we will explore every facet of visualization, and my goal is to leave you with a sound set of principles that will ensure that your clear thinking and systematic approach come through loud and clear and in living color for all to see.

Crafting an Effective Visualization

The objective of any problem solver is to tell a story by inviting our user to observe a visual replica of the system *in motion*—as in over time.

Visualizations play a critically important job in bringing the human brain into the model-understand-plan-act loop. The human brain is far better at pattern recognition than any computer we've ever devised.[1]

Of all of the activities that go into problem solving, visualization is likely one of the most creative, as it relies on your own thinking about how to best represent a system. However, you can easily build a bad visualization, so sound design principles do apply. You can steer your user's focus to a particular aspect of the system (that's good) and also unintentionally deceive (that's bad). It is a tricky proposition, one that comes with sober responsibilities.

Much like the discussion of Occam's razor in Chapter 1, our philosophy for visualization is to fairly represent the system with a *minimum* of elements. Think of a map of your city. The map by design leaves off certain details—the precise bend of a road or a grove of trees. As a map reader, all you care about is the route from one location to another. If these elements were added, the map would be more realistic, yes, but its ability to communicate the salient details would be compromised.

The converse is also often true—there are details that are invisible in the real world that must be brought forward in visualization. If you are working on a problem in a bank, for example, many of the flows of money and information from one end of the enterprise to the next are invisible in the real world, but can easily be made visible in our visualization of the system. The same is true for the flow of cases through a legal system, natural gas in a pipeline, or the spread of disease across a population.

Starting the Design Process

Good design starts by asking questions:

1. What kind of system am I representing? Is it a physical system like a supply chain, or is it a logical system like a communications network?

2. Is it important to represent the real system, or is a statistical summary or profile all that is needed?

3. If I observed the system over time, what kinds of changes would I see?

4. Is my objective to compare one system state to another? How should I do that comparison?

5. What is the cadence (time pacing) of the system? Would it be more insightful to speed up or slow down this real-world pace?

6. Who are the primary *actors* in the system? Upon what *stage* do they perform?

7. Are the relationships between the objects important? Should we highlight those relationships by drawing or labeling the connections between them?

8. Does my hypothesis hold clues as to which details should be emphasized and which can be ignored?

Over time, you will develop a knack for asking the right questions at the outset, and the answers will drive you to create a set of hand-drawn mock-ups for critique by the project team. These mock-ups are an essential artifact of the design process—don't shortcut this vital step.

Adding Design Elements to the Mock-up

You have designed visuals before—and you know that using just the right font and color and graphic form is important. But if you actually put in a bit more time, you will be surprised at the impact your story will have. Below are the basics (and a refresher for some) on what goes into the design elements of your story.

Many of these may sound like frivolous minutiae—but I can assure you that, taken together, these elements make for a professional look that draws your audience in. Have you ever heard anyone say, "I know a great piece of art when I see it, but I can't really tell you the precise features that separate great art from bad art"? That person is describing the carefully crafted graphic design principles that we will show you now.

Color Me Happy

Color is one of those elements that can make or break a good visual. PowerPoint, like many other graphics tools, allows you to make horrible graphics quickly and easily in just a few clicks.

Here are some general guidelines for the use of color, either in dynamic animations or in static images, or even in your qualitative model graphics:

- The warm part of the color spectrum (red, yellow, orange) is reserved for lightweight highlights, like thin hollow circles around an object or small location dots. Never use this color range for large-volume objects or text.
- If your graphic requires multiple color delineations, such as contiguous areas on a map, try first using several shades of the same color before using multiple colors. This is preferred even above gradient color collections (like a heat map in a range from red to blue), because it is less taxing on the brain in understanding the data.
- If you must use multiple colors, keep them to an absolute minimum and use pastel shades versus a bold, primary color—for example, pale light blue as opposed to bright blue. Use colors that tend to complement each other—light pink and light purple, for example, are too similar, but light pink goes very well with light gray.
- Text is almost always black on a light background or white on a dark background. Don't get cute with text color just because you can.

The Right Font for the Times

The most common violation of bad taste in graphic design that I see is in the selection of fonts. When I question teams, asking, "Why did you use Arial for that piece of text?" they sometimes look at me as if to say, "Oh, I have a choice of fonts? I just use whichever default font is set by my application." Tisk, tisk. If they only realized how important a font was to the brain's absorption of the material, they might not be so lackadaisical.

Fortunately, the choice of font is not a difficult one, in spite of the huge number of fonts we have loaded in our computers. Essentially Roman characters come in two major breeds, serif and sans serif. Serif fonts include extra bits on the characters. For example, use the Times or Times Roman font and blow up the capital letter "C." Do you see the little tick marks at the top and bottom ends of the curve? Those are serifs, and are widely considered to ease the brain's comprehension of large passages of text (paragraph and greater). Sans Serif fonts do not have these extra bits, and are therefore better for very short phrases—less than a sentence, such as in titles and labels.

Choice of typeface is up to you, although a few guidelines do apply. First, avoid using bizarre, exotic fonts in case your design ends up on the Web and your browser struggles to render it. Be relatively consistent from one project to the next, but don't be so rigid that you fail to modernize your collection every now and then, much like changing your clothes to meet a modern style (check out what typefaces major software companies and media outlets use). Arial, for example, has been used to death on computers for almost 30 years now, and is widely considered outdated in design circles.

Table 4.1 shows a range of typefaces and their strengths and weaknesses.

Once you choose a typeface, don't mix several on the same graphic—use only one. If you need emphasis or discrimination, use weight (bold or plain), size, or capitalization.

Dimensions—1D, 2D, 3D, or 4D?

There aren't just two dimensions out there in screenland any more. You have 3D, and even 4D (3D with motion) at your disposal, and you should use extra dimensions where necessary and appropriate. Conversely, 1D (horizontal time lines) is an option. The key point is to recognize your subject and match the aspects of that to the dimensions in your visual.

Table 4.1 Typefaces and their attributes

Typeface	Comments
Calibri	Good all-around modern looking font. Bolds well, and is even acceptable for long passages in spite of being Sans Serif
Gill Sans	One of the most beautiful typefaces around, and makes for a very professional look. Does not bold or italicize well, however.
Helvetica	This utility player has been around a very long time and still works. The best typeface for VERY large text, such as a number on a scorecard that is dynamically updated
Arial	Steer away from Arial—outdated and is the default font everywhere. Do you want your work to be like everyone else who doesn't try as hard?
Times, Times New, or Times New Roman	Heavy serifs make this good for long passages (paragraph or greater) only

Only 1D is highly specialized—generally reserved for systems that unfold over time, where the events observed in the system and the timing of these events is significant. In my own practice, I recall analyzing cases of wire fraud where the theft of funds from online brokerage accounts took place over many months, each event in sequence, labeled on the timeline in detail, leading up to the final point at which the funds were actually taken. Usually, 1D is combined with other visuals, but should not be ignored as a useful visual frame for time-paced systems.

You should not consider 2D the default frame whereby you need to be convinced to add another dimension. Rather, you should weigh 3D for its advantages, just as any other frame, particularly in light of the easy-to-use software tools we have now for representing 3D space (more on tools in the next chapter).

With 3D, you can zoom and pan to the area and angle of interest, which is particularly important for systems where the audience is diverse and seeks to view the portion of the system that they wish to see—micro or macro and everywhere in between. Also, 3D allows generous use of the concept I call *data adjacency*.

For well over 15 years, professional football fans in the United States have been treated to an exercise in data adjacency. The so-called "first and ten" line that shows the yardage point the team must get the ball to, in order to gain a first down is superimposed on the field. This is a classic example of data adjacency where you have the physical scene (the game and the field), combined with an expressed piece of data (the first down line) in order to enhance the viewer's understanding of the system (many other sports around the world now use some form of this). Watching one of these games, you get a very immediate sense of the distance to the first down, and that's the point—to combine data with adjacent physical objects so that pattern recognition is enhanced. In a business context, think of a collection of stores in a geographic region splayed across a map, and vertical bars next to each one whose Z-dimension height is proportional to sales. With this kind of portrayal, you would get an instant sense of the pattern of sales—the biggest, the smallest, and everywhere in between.

With 4D, the motion concept is added to 3D, evolution over time. Does motion enhance your audience's appreciation of the system? I like to think of it as analogous to a "day in the life" of the system. If you could watch a day in the life of the system as it unfolds, minute by minute, hour by hour (perhaps at 10X speed), would that reveal insights that you would not have with a static 3D portrayal?

Production systems are classic examples of systems in motion. By ripping the roof off of a factory and peering into it, you see all the workflows and assemblies moving from one station to another as the units are built. Keep in mind, however, the broader definition of a production system— this could include banks, insurance companies—places where the real-world workflow is invisible, but is made visible with your visualization of it. Clearly, watching these systems over time as queues build up, traffic is rerouted, and items move at different rates or get rerouted backward for rework is far more revealing than a static picture.

Use of 3D and beyond does come with some overhead—you now have to be conscious of camera angle and position and the lighting of the scene. However, these aspects are not difficult to control once you have mastered the visualization tools themselves.

Tooltipping

Most visualization software allows for a "tooltips" feature—hovering the mouse over an object to reveal an additional, more detailed description of that object. Tooltips are an excellent way to create space efficiency in the visualization, and I would encourage generous use of them, particularly in those cases where the objects are, by necessity, identified by short codes.

Highlighting

Not all objects in your system are treated equally. Some require a special status to which you want to draw attention, and you do so in visualizations through a technique known as highlighting. As the name implies, we use additional elements to discriminate certain objects. In the case of 4D, this could be a yellow circle that is drawn around one piece of workflow that stays with that item throughout its life in the scene as it moves. For 2D graphs, this could be a particular data point that is specially colored red, or perhaps has a text annotation above it with a line connecting the two. In any case, highlighting is an important mechanism for elevating certain features of the visual.

There are no hard-and-fast rules for highlighting, but be cautious about overdoing highlighting. It is possible that you might draw the attention of your audience so much to particular features that they ignore other important aspects. Just ask yourself a question: am I using highlighting generally, or is there a clear and unequivocal reason why certain objects have special status?

Special Cases

Certain systems have signature features that lend themselves well to particular styles of visual representation. One can certainly deviate from these suggested styles, but they are nevertheless highly useful as a starting point for design.

Geographic Maps

I'll admit to a particular obsession with geographic maps. I could stare at them for hours. A great map is like a work of art—the more you look at it, the more intrigued you become. I don't think I am alone in this fascination with maps, and you as an analyst should use their popularity wisely in your designs.

Here are ways to use maps correctly in your visualizations:

1. The minimalist principle applies. Just the features of the map that are needed to tell the story, and nothing more. For example, do you *really* need a topographic map, or is a plain flat one sufficient? Do streets distract or add value?

2. Color is important. Use a simple color palette. It is best to use multiple shades of the same color first, before using multiple colors. If you have mixed land and water on your map, use a green shade for land and a blue shade for water as necessary to prevent confusion for the user (this last point may sound trivial, but you would be amazed at how many times it is violated in the real world). Map highlights such as landmarks or routes should use the warm part of the color spectrum (red, yellow, orange).

3. Use mapping software tools that allow for zoom-dependent detail.

4. Don't assume that your audience knows your specific landmarks. Include common landmarks (like major cities, bodies of water, or well-known highways) along with your data if possible.

5. Always use a "North-Up" orientation, and label as such.

Process Flow

A system that moves work items from one state to another, and then another is a process flow system, continuous in the case of a chemical plant, and discrete in the case of a automobile factory. In either case, the objective of a process flow system is to transform objects or material in one state into a finished state through a set of interlinked process steps. Processes can be physical, as in a material supply chain, or they can be logical, like the processing of insurance claims. A process orientation is the cornerstone of *lean thinking*,[2] which is a "second cousin" to business problem solving. Moreover, processes are all around us in every corner of the economy. Representing these correctly is critically important for the problem solver.

The two fundamental elements of process systems are the processes themselves and the flows between them. Processes, by definition, perform a transformation on some input to derive an output. It is an action, and therefore should be labeled using a verb phrase, in title case. For example, "Verify Phone Number" is an appropriate label for a process, while "Phone Number" is not. The shape of a process should always be rectangular, and, if filled with color, use a light pastel palette from the cool part of the color spectrum (blue, green, purple). The border should be of the same color family, but at least 2 shades darker.

Process depictions also need to adhere to some standards in order to be effective.[3] I recommend the so-called ICOM standard from the $IDEF_0$ functional modeling framework.[4] ICOM stands for inputs, controls, outputs, and mechanisms, and it works very simply: inputs should always come into a process on its left-hand side. Outputs should extend from the right. Controls, those elements that influence the input-to-output conversion in the same way that a "recipe" influences the process "Make a Cake," come in to the top of the process rectangle. Mechanisms are the resources that are used in the process, like "mixer" and "baking pan" in our cake example, and these come in to the bottom of the rectangle. Adhering to these standards will make your visuals much more readable.

Flow lines should always be labeled, and because there are "things" flowing, it is important to label them with noun phrases, in lower case. An appropriate label for a flow is "baked cake." Arrowheads should terminate the flow lines, and you should avoid double-headed arrows in favor of two separate unidirectional lines. The lines should be at least two points thicker than the borders of the process flow rectangles.

Process diagrams should be arranged where the flow is generally from the left side of the page to the right side of the page, NOT from top to bottom. Chaining—restarting a process flow on the left side of the page in a lower row as you run out of room on the right side—is perfectly acceptable.

Once you have a process depicted, putting it in motion often involves workflow items moving from one process to the next across the flow lines. Tiny spheres (3D) or filled circles (2D) in warm colors tend to work best.

Sources and Uses

It is a common objective to show the connection between a volume of "stuff" on the one hand, and how that stuff is distributed to a series of pigeonholes on the other hand. This arises in capital structure models of money flows or supply/demand configurations, such as production chains where N factories produce products for M distribution centers. Sankey diagrams accomplish this representation very nicely, and in our own work we use them rather frequently.

Named for Irish sea captain Matthew H. P. R. Sankey, who first used the format to illustrate the energy flows in a steam engine,[5] Sankey diagrams illustrate a left-hand side volume of sources that splits across a right-hand side set of uses as shown in Figure 4.1. One can further make use of color discrimination in the flows for categorization.

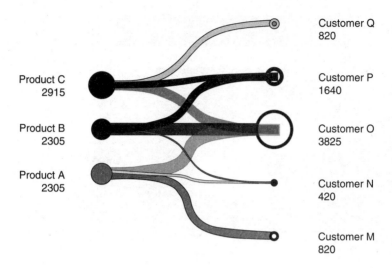

Figure 4.1 A Sankey diagram example

Capacity

So often, we work on problems that involve the capacity of something—the capacity of a unit of transportation like a ship or a truck or a pipeline, the capacity of a communications or data storage system, or even capacity in the form of a financial budget. With fixed limits on something, the problem involves visualizing the diverse use of that capacity and all of the complex elements that entails.

An effective instrument for representing capacity and its utilization is the treemap.[6] In its simplest form, a treemap is a square, and the square is divided into a variety of regions, with the area of each region proportional to that item's use of the capacity, represented by the whole of the square. Therefore, if you had a treemap of a government's federal budget, one region would be health care, another would be defense, another would be education, and so on. The shape of the regions is irrelevant (and is worked out by an algorithm). The important feature is the *area* of each consumer object. The rules regarding the color of the treemap regions change a bit here: since we have large numbers of tessellating regions, it is perfectly acceptable to use a widely diverse primary color palette across the warm-to-cool color range (see Figure 4.2)

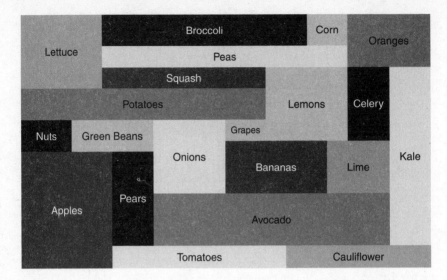

Figure 4.2 A treemap showing the proportional shelf space consumption of items in the produce section of a food market

A question you might ask at this stage is, "Can't I do the same thing with a stacked bar?" The answer is yes, and we routinely use stacked bars in our own work for representing capacity. However, there is one distinct advantage to treemaps: they do not imply some kind of order or sequence, whereas stacked bars lead the audience to believe that the top-to-bottom arrangement of the stack means something when it often does not.

The same comment can be applied to pie charts. In general, pie chart representations of any data element are very difficult to read and force the brain to do far too much processing in order to compare elements. Do not use pie charts when there are so many other good alternatives.

Scenarios

Often your hypothesis question will be, "How does my organization/ asset/project fare in a wide variety of future scenarios?" Scenarios are most often thought of as external events or conditions that are not under your organization's control, such as competitive actions or the health of the economy. On another front, you may have a number of mutually exclusive decisions to make—strategies, if you will—and the goal is to choose the right strategy among a large number of choices. A model of some sort determines the quantitative performance of the system for each decision against each scenario.

In chapter 1, we introduced the idea of robustness, the modern way of looking at corporate strategy. Robustness is a lens through which we clearly see that one strategy is superior to another because it works well in a wide variety of scenarios versus working spectacularly well in only a few. Strategic thinking is enhanced when we use a *strategy matrix* to portray scenarios (see Figure 4.3).

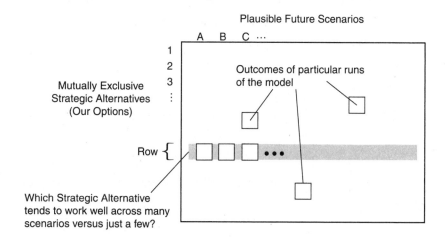

Figure 4.3 The strategy matrix

To construct a strategy matrix, lay out the columns of a table as the scenarios—those external forces that will test your strategy in a unique sort of way. The rows of the table are the mutually exclusive decisions—the strategies under your control. The cells at the intersection of the two are the quantitative outputs of your model, the inputs mapping to the decision and the scenario. The cells are best expressed as a graph or graphic for readability.

When scenarios are framed in this way, the row-wise robustness of a given strategy becomes very clear.

Tables

Tables are fundamental to the organization of complex information, and it is surprising how often they are portrayed badly. The general rules for table visualization are as follows:

1. Use a solid dark field background in the cool color range (blue, purple, or gray, but not black) for the header, with bold white text. Title text should be 2 points larger than the body text.
2. If you are using both a column header and a row header, make the background of the row headers 2–3 shades lighter than the column header, using the same color. Row titles should be bold black.
3. Body or cell text should always be black against a white background.
4. Fonts should be sans serif throughout.
5. Avoid using lines that delimit the columns. A generous amount of white space will give your users the necessary separation between columns without drawing lines. Rows on the other hand should be delimited with thin black border lines.
6. Keep any one piece of cell text as short (character count) as possible. If you find that you have multiple paragraphs for text, consider tooltipping, as described above. Your aim is for balance across your table—no one cell should have far more text than another. Balance enhances readability.
7. The table designer should make the choice of sorting the table or not, but if sorted, always indicate as such.

Decision Trees

A second cousin of the scenarios above is the *decision tree*, where decisions unfold over a series of steps. The starting point at the trunk of the tree is the initial state of the system. The initial state is confronted with two or more mutually exclusive choices. Each choice then brings the system to another state, where two or more new mutually exclusive choices are imperative. The cycle repeats again and again until you reach a leaf—a point at which you have reached a final state with no more decisions to make.

As in scenarios, a model drives the content of a decision tree. Each state after the initial one is the output of a model that uses the branch from the previous state as a set of input parameters reflecting the choice of that particular decision. Visually, a state should be shown as a solid pastel-colored rectangle or circle, as this lines up well with an indeterminate number of thin black decision arrows that extend from it. A graphic representing the state—a plot or a mini table of metrics or both—can be shown just below the circle. The orientation of the tree should always be left to right, as if the tree has fallen over to the right side. Never extend decision trees across multiple pages; rather, use a very large single page if necessary (see Figure 4.4).

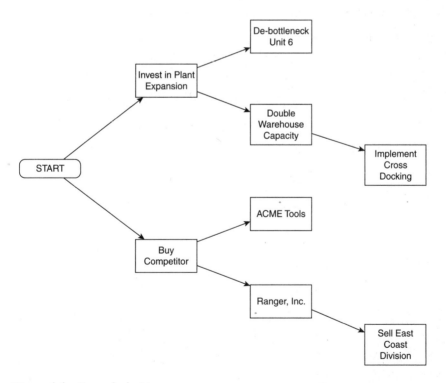

Figure 4.4 Example decision tree

Decision trees can be a particularly useful way to show how decisions evolve over time. New information learned at each branch can clarify later branches or add altogether new branches to the tree. For extra clarity label the nodes with information about what the state of the system will be at this stage, and label the branches with the action(s) that cause the movement from one node to another. Best practice is to maintain updates to the trees as frequently as new information arises to make it into a working document.

Animation

Perhaps one of the most important ideas to emerge in the visualization of complex systems is animation—quite literally, building a movie of a system as it operates over time. Animation underscores the philosophy of inviting the human analyst into the problem-solving loop, as opposed to shutting them out with a fortress built on opaque nests of calculations. Most humans are visual, and animation is among the highest forms of visual communication. The best news of all is that animation, once very difficult and time consuming, is now far easier to achieve than ever before. It should be part of every problem solver's visual toolbox.

Thinking through an animation design that relates to your problem requires consideration of two central elements: the scene and the actors. The scene is the environment in which the animation sits, so perhaps a supply chain problem uses a map of the countries across which product movements occur, or in the case of a process problem, it is the depiction of the processes and flows of work among them. Generally speaking, the scene is a set of elements in the animation that sets a context, but does not change over time, like the set of a theatrical production.

The actors are the dynamic elements that move and change over time. The audience's eyes will focus on the actors. If your problem is a factory, the work items and perhaps the factory workers will be actors. In a bank, tranches of cash and other transaction objects will be actors, moving from one account or process to another.

In the early days of computer simulation, we only had a choice of 2D animations, typically a "plan view" overhead of some factory-like process where small tokens representing products moved around on the screen from one end to another across the plumbing of the factory. Today, it is easy to generate 3D renderings of these kinds of systems, and we should take advantage of the additional fidelity that 3D provides: zoom and pan, perspective, and perhaps most important, data adjacency, which we introduced in chapter 3. Data adjacency is the act of placing a purely data element (like a vertical bar whose height is proportional to a measured attribute), in close proximity with an object in a physical scene.

Animation provides us with a means to alter the real world to the benefit of our audience. For example, most systems in the real world operate at a certain pace—very slowly or very quickly. We would not want our audience to view "a day in the life" of a process at real-time speeds. With animation, we can control the time pacing and set it suitably for the audience to see the patterns effectively.

There are a surprising number of real-world systems where the key elements are invisible: banking, which deals with flows of money; pipelines in which natural gas flows, or criminal justice systems that process cases. Once again, in the simulated world we can alter the features and make the invisible visible. Flows of invisible things can become representative "tokens" that appear in the animation and move in accordance with their real-world counterparts.

In designing animations for your audience, always keep in mind one thing: where are my audience's eyes going? There should always be a central focus on the page—too much activity randomly scattered can be distracting and confusing.

Storytelling with Your Visualization

After applying the design guidelines to create a working visualization, you are now in a position to assimilate the design into a truly effective visual story. We do this by carefully applying any one or more of the three fundamental aspects of graphical illustration: juxtaposition, relative analysis, and hierarchy.

Juxtaposition

Placing two like elements together is a very powerful way to make comparisons. In analytics, this involves two instances of visualization that are driven by small differences in two model input sets. The need for juxtaposition arises often in analysis where you want to show the impact of making some change to a system, as in an "As-Is" (how the system works now) versus a "To-Be" (how the system performs when the change is introduced, everything else held constant).

Showing the As-Is visual immediately followed by the To-Be visual will allow your audience to see the differences clearly. In fact, I have seen cases where the As-Is and the To-Be are shown side by side on the same screen for maximum impact.

Relative Analysis

What if we could go back in time, make a change to our system, and relive history with that change in place? We can, using a technique known as *relative analysis*.

Often we find ourselves with historical data about a system's performance. A hospital emergency room (ER), for example, has very detailed information about which patients were seen, at which times, with which conditions, the attending physician, the treatment given—near minute-by-minute breakdowns of the operation in data. If our problem is, say, to determine the impact of the addition of one more doctor to the ER, we could build our model to work from historical data showing two cases: (1) As-Is—how the ER *actually performed* in week 20 last year, and (2) To Be—how the hospital *would have performed* had we added one more doctor.

Relative analysis provides a more compelling case to your audience than a simple future forecast because its starting point is the actual system's performance at a given period in time.

Hierarchy

Eagerness and enthusiasm to tell a story behind the solution to a problem can lead an analyst to include too many elements in a visualization at one time. Remember the audience, and understand that the brain processes the information in stages, small chunks at a time. If your chunk has too many elements, the brain will not comprehend the full story and all of your good work will be lost. We can fix this with hierarchy, as shown in Figure 4.5.

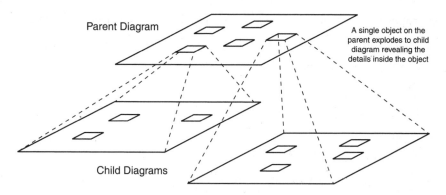

Figure 4.5   Using hierarchies to contextualize and focus the level of detail

As the name implies, hierarchy meters how much the audience is exposed to at any given time, yet organizes the chunks in a way that the brain can digest them in a logical, deliberate sequence. I recall a situation from our own work where we were asked to analyze the performance of a large chemical production complex, which was actually three plants in one, each plant containing up to a half-dozen individual units. This organization of the physical system allowed us to mirror that in our visualization—we showed the whole complex as a black box to start, but clicking on that object showed the three connected plants, and then clicking on each plant revealed the units, and so on. In the end we showed the entire facility's performance in exhaustive detail, but we did so by directing our audience's brains to focus on specific pieces at a time, while underscoring the connections between each in a very straightforward way.

Chapter Summary

Before reading this book, you may have had the misguided notion that solving a problem was all that was needed to...solve the problem. You now know that this is only half the journey—we must also communicate our solution to a broad audience of stakeholders who are not intimately familiar with your approach, nor are skilled in analysis. We use visualization to accomplish this. Great care and handling go into the creation of a bespoke visualization that shows just the elements of your solution, without unnecessary and distracting details. Follow a few foundational design principles and you are well on your way to communicating complex solutions effectively with your audience.

In these chapters we have covered many things—applying mathematical methods, handling data, visualizing systems. None of this can be done without software applications. What tools do I use? When do I apply one software tool versus another? How do I get them all to work together?

These questions and many more will be the subject of the next chapter, in which we discuss the tools of the trade.

CHAPTER 5

Tools of the Trade: The Technology of Problem Solving

The world of the elite athlete is fascinating. In my professional life I have come into contact with some extremely gifted athletes—the kind of performers who dominate their sport, setting the bar far higher than the second best in the world. Having observed these amazing humans in action, I have noticed one thing that distinguishes the elite athlete from just simply the world-class athlete—an obsession, with the tools of their sport. Olympic swimmers fuss over their swimsuits, tennis players seek a oneness with their rackets, and professional jockeys fiddle endlessly with their saddles. And let's not even talk about race car drivers and their cars.

These athletes have recognized that the tools of their trade are the key to the position they hold in a highly competitive world, where a hair's breadth of advantage can mean the difference between number 1 and number 37. They spare no expense in acquiring the very best tools, and even work closely with equipment manufacturer's research and development groups to push the envelope of performance year after year.

The same should be the case for organizations. Problem solving in one form or another is one of the most important components of work; therefore, the tools we apply to those problems should be the best that they can be. Sadly, this is rarely the case. "Just use Excel because... that's what we have and it's already paid for" is a phrase I have heard far too many times in working with companies. But this can be a dangerous attitude. In this chapter I will share with you how to develop proficiency in a range of software tools for problem solving so that the tool is matched, in a "no compromise" way, precisely to the problem at hand.

Now We're Cooking

Any good cook brings three elements together before turning on the stove. First, there is the selection of the recipe—the instructions that will guide the process (although deviations from the recipe are common). Second, there are the ingredients, the raw materials to be added to the meal at just the right time in deliberate amounts. And finally there are the tools of cooking—ovens, knives, bowls, spoons, mixers, stoves—the mechanisms of the cooking process. The very best chefs prestage these elements to drive out any "friction" in the seamless movements from one step to another.

So it is with problem solving. Our recipe is the qualitative model that we've crafted from a preceding hypothesis step. The ingredients are data, arranged in a database form for easy extraction. The cooking tools are the computational software platforms and languages in which our model code runs to generates results. Like the master chef, we will prestage all of these elements in ways that make problem solving fast, efficient, and of high quality. IT professionals refer to this as a reference architecture for analytics, a permanent facility for housing every software component that one might need to solve a problem from beginning to end. Let's start by looking conceptually at what the architecture might include, starting with four broad categories of components (see Figure 5.1).

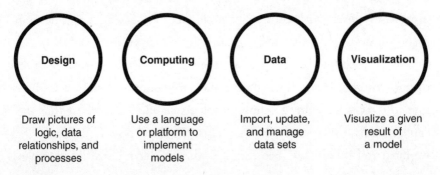

Design	Computing	Data	Visualization
Draw pictures of logic, data relationships, and processes	Use a language or platform to implement models	Import, update, and manage data sets	Visualize a given result of a model

Figure 5.1 Categories of problem-solving components

Design is one of the most overlooked parts of the solver's toolset, yet the ability to draw pictures is one of the most important subtasks we do in problem solving. In particular, we look for a drawing tool that implements layering—putting objects in various virtual layers that can be turned on or off, revealing different aspects of the system from a single graphic.

The *computing* environment provides a language for describing the system in code, based upon the blueprint generated using the design tools.

Handling *data*, particularly large or multiple data sets, is a job for tools built specifically for this task.

Visualization tools work with the results of models (and sometimes their associated data) to portray the result in a graphical or perhaps animated interactive form.

Bench Strength

It is important to identify these categories as independent but interconnected sets of functions because many organizations unwisely seek to stretch a given tool across multiple categories. It is perfectly acceptable—and in fact expected—that there will be multiple choices of tools in each of these categories to allow the problem solvers to match the collection of tools to the problem at hand. No one problem is ever the same; therefore, we should not expect that any one particular tool or tool set will handle the entire range. "Tool bending"—unnaturally applying a tool to the wrong function—is poor practice, and will result in suboptimal performance of the solution overall. Let me dispel two notions that are often the culprits behind tool-bending:

Myth 1: "My People Can't Learn to Be Proficient in More Than One Tool"
If this is true, you have the wrong people (that's the subject of a coming chapter), or you are over estimating the challenge of learning new (but similar) tools. Most problem-solving teams can adapt well to tools across the 4-space in Figure 5.1, and in doing so create the benefit of making each contributor a better, more flexible solver. Software offerings come and go—so rigidly adhering to one language or application in any case is risky business.

Myth 2: "It's Too Expensive to Buy and Maintain Wide Range of Tools"
The cost of the tools relative to the financial magnitude of the problems that flow through them should be very, very small. If that is not the case,

you are working on the wrong problems, or your budgets for software are not aligned with the priorities of the business in a "penny wise, pound foolish" sort of way.

I have seen in my own practice projects completely fall apart because the wrong tools were applied to the problem.

A Workflow for Problem Solving

When we solve problems, there is a sequence at work. Process-minded folks call this *workflow*, and it defines the plumbing that a problem goes through from beginning to end. With this in mind, let is look at a structure for implementing any conceivable problem-solving workflow, in light of the four classes we mentioned earlier. An example is shown in Figure 5.2.

The Role and Function of Design

Design is typically the first environment engaged in the problem-solving process. Based upon the business problem and in consultation with SMEs, a hypothesis is generated, followed quickly by a series of images that together comprise the qualitative model. This forms the blueprint that the solver will use to create the code for the model. Alongside this effort comes the data model,[1] which is also a graphical depiction of the data objects and their relationships, which can be thought of in simplest form as tables and keys (data modeling was discussed in chapter 3). Like the qualitative model, the data model is a guide for the solver to set up the table structure to house the model's data.

We have found that technical drawing applications that support layering and hierarchy work best for design (see Figure 5.3). Microsoft Visio (Windows only), Omnigraffle (Mac only), and Adobe Illustrator (both) each do this, but given that the software landscape changes rather frequently please see this book's companion website at http://www.business-laboratory.com/profitfromscience.

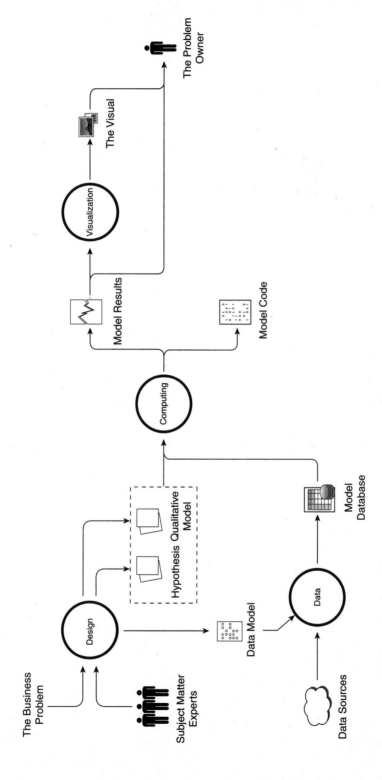

Figure 5.2 Problem-solving workflow

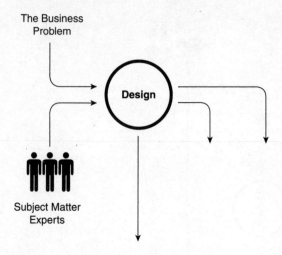

Figure 5.3 Design

Layering is the assignment of graphical objects to layers that can be turned on and off. For example, let's say you had a process flow diagram illustrating the sequence of activities in a manufacturing plant or an insurance company. Along with that depiction, there are several text comments about certain regions in the diagram; however, there is so much text that the comments cover up important pieces of the underlying diagram. In this is case, turning the comments on and off in a layer can be very handy.

The principle of hierarchy comes into play when you create a series of diagrams in which there is one main, high-level diagram at the top, and objects on that main diagram "explode" into a whole separate diagram with more detail about that object. The explosions then in turn generate more explosions themselves in increasing levels of detail until the entire system is exhaustively depicted through the tree network of illustrations.

Returning to the process map example, there is a parent object called "process order" on a diagram of equivalent objects at that level. However, clicking on process order reveals a whole new diagram of how that parent works internally. Using hierarchy, you are never forced as a designer to put way too much detail on any given page, an important principle of readability.

A "nice to have" feature in the design tool is a gallery of prebuilt stencils that can be applied to a drawing and modified as needed. Typically these stencil galleries are organized by type of drawing—flow chart, mind map, software—for faster selection.

From Data Model to Database

The data environment encompasses all the tools necessary to move from the data model (effectively the database on paper) to a working data repository that feeds the computational models (see Figure 5.4). There are three primary components to this function: ETL, a so-called "ad hoc" database utility, and the relational database system itself.

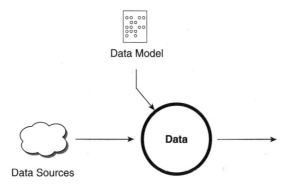

Data Model

Data

Data Sources

Figure 5.4 Database design

ETL is a formal description of utilities designed to move data from a data source, be it a corporate database, a website, or a local file, to a format in the model database that is readily usable by the model. ETL can be as sophisticated as a routinely scheduled task that moves many files from various locations while performing sophisticated data conversions, or as simple as the manual upload of a spreadsheet.

It is hard to beat the spreadsheet for data cleansing and preparation—its flexibility is well suited to transposing, aggregating, reformatting, and filtering—all fundamental operations of data preparation. Once the data is in a clean and organized form, most database management systems readily accept a spreadsheet as an import format.

The ad hoc utility takes care of development-related tasks such as table creation, data import from text files and spreadsheets (and other databases), and updates. The database system is the target for all of the data the models will use, and respond to query statements with data extracts—tabular results that correspond to a query. The model software communicates to the database over Internet protocols.

There is a wide range of choices available for the database system, ranging from simple to sophisticated. At the simple end of the spectrum we have spreadsheets—in which each tab is a table of data. An alternative to a local spreadsheet file is a Google Spreadsheet document. It is the same form as a spreadsheet, but because it is online and shared, there is never a question of which version of multiple copies of a file is the correct one. Google Spreadsheets also have more rigorous version controls. A Google Spreadsheet by a model can be accessed through a simple unique URL link that Google provides.

Microsoft Access is one of several desktop database systems that support the structured query language (SQL). SQL support allows for the data to be filtered and formatted, as in *"give me the sales from the south region where the sales manager was Jane."* Desktop database applications are popular, and include their own built-in ad hoc utilities, but do have size and performance limitations that prevent them from scaling to large datasets easily.

Most often, the correct long-term choice for a database system is a full-scale relational database management system such as Microsoft SQL Server, Oracle, or MySQL. These systems are designed for very large data sets and have a substantial set of features geared to high performance, reliability, and multiple simultaneous user access.

Most organizations have at least one of these kinds of systems for performing production IT tasks. For problem solving, and especially sandbox-oriented use of databases, it is often convenient to use a cloud-based pay-as-you-go service versus purchasing and installing a database system to run on a corporate server. Amazon, Rackspace, and Microsoft are just a few of the many options for cloud-based data services.

Computation

It's no accident that the computation function is literally at the center of the workflow. This is where "modeling" happens with code, where the logic of the real system is replicated and executed (see Figure 5.5).

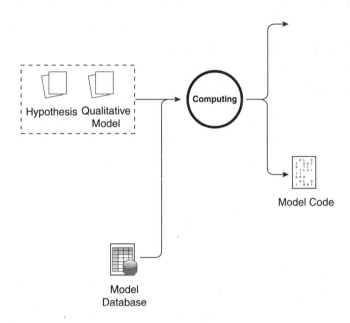

Figure 5.5 Computing

The most flexible environments for computation are software languages that lend themselves well to mathematical functions and simulation. That includes general purpose languages such as C# and Java, and also math-specific languages like *Mathematica* (or Wolfram Language), Matlab, R, and SAS.

Less flexible but more purpose-built applications like Promodel, FlexSim, and Simul8 hide much of the code from the user in place of "drag and drop objects, then connect them together"—style interfaces. Other applications like Tableau, SpotFire, and QlikView offer rapid development graphical depictions of data that has been "dropped" into the application.

There are many, many fine software tools in the analytics world that I haven't mentioned here—the ones I have highlighted are intended to serve as category examples.[2] The application or language that you choose is a matter of, in some cases, personal taste. However, in the many years I have been working in the problem-solving domain, one thing is certain—the diversity of problems that will come your way will constantly surprise you; therefore, flexibility in the computation environment is absolutely essential. Flexibility will tend to favor lower-level languages in which the model is built up from code through programming.

Flexibility does not only mean agility in the face of diverse problems but also applies to scale. What if that factory you are modeling turns into ten factories worldwide? What if the data aggregated by zip code becomes data on each and every individual? It is very common for a pilot-scale model or underlying data or both to jump to 10X in subsequent phases. Will your language handle that with grace and speed, or will it grind to a halt? Good languages have features that adapt to step changes in scale.

Unit Testing

It is quite helpful if your language has a convenient unit-testing feature. Unit testing is the isolation of particular code fragments where you can give each fragment a particular set of inputs and test against an expected set of outputs. The tests fail if the isolated code fragment output that does not match the expected output. More sophisticated unit tests allow developers to express a pattern as an output, such as "a list of 10 numbers, all of which are positive real numbers less than 100."

Unit testing becomes very important in larger, more complex models. It is often the case that you make a change to the model in one area, and you want to make sure that change doesn't create errors in other parts of the model. Unit testing is a handy framework for quickly checking against errors introduced in this way.

Visualization

Visualization environments turn raw result data—usually numbers and strings—into visual representations with color, shape, and scale, each contributing to the audience's understanding of the expressed patterns in the results (see Figure 5.6). For example, Google Earth is an excellent 3D map-based application for showing photo-realistic views of the earth at a wide range of zoom angles, from outer space to your neighbor's backyard. We use Google Earth in our practice for almost all of our geocentric visualizations—airlines, supply chains, and political analysis. Visualizations in Google Earth can be static or animated over time. It includes extensive functionality for interactivity, allowing clickable subviews of objects on the map.

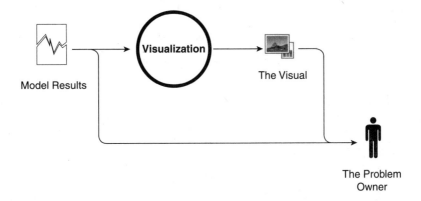

Figure 5.6 Visualization

Google Earth uses KML files to direct the rendering of the visualization. KML stands for Keyhole Markup Language, a nod to the company, Keyhole, that built the original application before they were bought by Google. KML is a derivation of XML, a universal standard for web-based file structures. Below is a sample of a KML file:

```
<?xml version="1.0" encoding="utf-8"?>
<kml xmlns="http://www.opengis.net/kml/2.2">
<Document>
<name>Balloon with image</name>
<Placemark>
<name>Image in balloon</name>
<description>
```

```
<![CDATA[
Here is an image:
<img src="images/googleearth.gif"/>
]]>
</description>
<Point>
<coordinates>-121.22,37.44</coordinates>
</Point>
</Placemark>
</Document>
</kml>
```

This very simple KML places an image at a particular latitude and longitude (lat/lon) on the earth.[3] If you ask Google Earth to open (the technical term is *consume*) this file, it will fly into where the placemark is located.

Let's say you've built a routing application that shows an optimal straight-line path for trucks to follow in sequence to ensure the fastest possible overall delivery. The nominal output of your model is likely a table of locations in delivery order from top to bottom, such as the example shown in Table 5.1.

Table 5.1 Stops along a delivery route

Stop Sequence	Location
1	Aurora
2	Blooming Hills
3	Eldergate
4	Joplindale
5	Dickerson
6	Highland Heights

If you wanted to show this route to others in a more compelling format, it would be a straightforward matter to develop some code to create a KML file from the table, with number placemarks on each stop and lines connecting each from-to pair (see example in Figure 5.7).

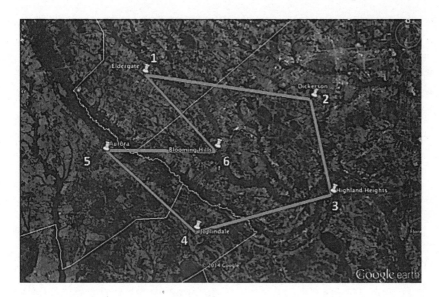

Figure 5.7   A map of the route sequence

While this example uses Google Earth as the target visualization application, the same approach is used in general for many visualization targets—create a special file or object from your results data that the visualization application can consume. Some input files follow a rather elaborate protocol, like Google Earth, while others require no more than a ".csv" (comma delimited text) format.

Tableau is one such application that requires a very simple format—.csv or Excel standard files. In addition, you must follow a few rules (no breaks in rows, no repeated headers, flattened data). Moving the data into Tableau then allows the solver to choose from a large gallery of pre-built visual forms or create a new one.

For situations that call for the animation of a complex "scene" with objects moving in coordinated ways, we increasingly rely on the video game industry to provide the tools. This industry spends great resources every year on the technology to render scenes very rapidly on a common browser with a high degree of realism. In recent years, the industry has put the basic engines for game development into the public domain for anyone to use. An example is Unity, one of the most popular game engines in the industry, distributed via open source.

Unity is a formidable system—it includes features for the control of lighting, camera angle, and movement. It provides a designer with the ability to implement a heads-up display (HUD) layer on top of the scene view. It can be programmed internally using languages like C# and Javascript. With all of this power comes a good deal of complexity. However, the payback from using Unity is tremendous—game-quality visualization with complete animation and interactivity.

Animation Express

If you want simple, noninteractive animation without the overhead of an environment like Unity, here is a trick you can use. We call it the frames method. Assuming your computing tools have the ability to draw a static image programmatically, set up your code to draw many, many static frames, each frame an image file showing the next increment of movement. The files should all be in one folder and all with a number indicating the sequence of frames: myMovie1.jpg, myMovie2.jpg, and so on. Apple's Quicktime Pro can then load all of these images and produce a smooth Quicktime movie from the result.

The Sandbox Concept

Most organizations of any size have an IT department, even if this "department" is actually outsourced to another company. IT maintains control over the production systems—the software that glues the company's information together as it conducts a normal course of business every day, hence the term "production."

Analytical computing for problem solving is a very different beast. It is an ad hoc, opportunistic, play-it-as-it comes, experiment-and-fail-many-times kind of game. However, because it is computing and technology, many have come to believe that it belongs in the IT department, or should use IT resources. This sounds mildly sensible, but it is just plain wrong.

It is far better to think of problem solvers as playing in a "sandbox"—a creative playground with randomly scattered toys, free of the rules that keep you from getting yourself or others into trouble (as long as you stay in that sandbox!). Occasionally, the grown-ups need to fill the sandbox with fresh sand and replace a few broken toys, but other than that, the solvers keep going.

We recommend that the technical environment for problem solving be distinctly separate from the production IT environment, but connected in ways that allow data to be exported from production IT into the sandbox environment. Data can as well flow back into production IT, but most likely into a staging area of the database, ready for an ETL process to manage the import operation (see Figure 5.8).

Figure 5.8 One way ETL from production to the sandbox

Moreover the sandbox should be free of many of the IT restrictions that extend to users. Problem solvers will constantly wish to install new applications, code, and data, throw that away, and start all over again, all without having to fill out a form or plead to some bureaucrat for permission. What we are *not* suggesting is that the sandbox should be any less secure than production IT.

Over time, the sandbox will promote code reusability, as all models will be housed in the same virtual locale so that functions can be chained together to form compound functions.

The Special Case of Long-Running Models

On occasion you will build models that take hours or even days to run. This is especially prevalent in these days of big data, where even simple calculations spanning incredibly large data sets can extend the total run time.

Running such a model on a desktop machine is most often not practical unless the run is done overnight, as the model tends to lock up the machine against other uses. The better approach is to set up a virtual machine in the cloud for running these models, with alerts on completion or error.

Note that this approach also works well for models that must run at definite intervals without user interaction—such as a financial model that runs the first Monday of every month and automatically e-mails a result to the Finance team. This is known as a batch run, which can be set up to run in an unattended manner on a virtual server.

Now you might ask, "Why can't I just make the thing run faster?" You can. And in some cases, speeding up the model may eliminate the need for a batch-style run. There are three common techniques for speeding up long-running code: optimization, parallelization, and graphical processing unit (GPU) harnessing.

Code optimization involves the use of a code profiler that can tell you where the model is spending a majority of its time. With this information you can examine the particular code section to see if it can be streamlined for faster execution. Once this is completed, go to the next most common code section, and so on. It is not unusual to get 10X to 50X speed-ups simply by profiling the code and working on the bottlenecks.

Parallelization involves running a model on a "grid" of networked computers in which one master computer doles out pieces of the computation load to a number of subservient machines. Some languages compel the developer to set parallelization up manually, while others make execution on a grid fairly seamless and automatic. If you anticipate running very complex models across large data sets, be sure to examine the language's parallelization features carefully.

Finally, every desktop machine has two kinds of processors inside: a set of core central processing units (CPUs), and an array of graphical processing units (GPUs), typically on a separate video card, for displaying graphics. GPUs outnumber CPUs, allowing developers to hardware-accelerate certain applications. Conveniently, software architectures such as CUDA (developed by graphics card manufacturer nVidia) and OpenCL create a device-level interface to GPUs that many technical computing languages are now supporting.

Deployment

Moving a model, or any piece of software, for that matter, out of a development environment into an every-day-usage form is called deployment. If the problem solver is the only user of the model, this is not a necessary step. However, most all problems involve a variety of stakeholders and interested parties, so getting a model into the hands of users well outside of the developer's highly instrumented and technical world is necessary.

The goal is to create a form of the model that is highly intuitive and easy to access. Increasingly this means doing this through a common web browser. The better computing tools offer a seamless way to move from a mathematical programming environment to a Hypertext Markup Language (HTML) deployment target seamlessly, keeping any animation or interactivity for the user intact. *Mathematica*, for example, makes use of the computable document format (CDF) that can be embedded into any standard web page.

Make sure that whatever development environment you choose includes a well-defined path to deployment so that others can get access to your work.

Data Security

The security of data is on everyone's minds these days, with painful security breaches making the headlines routinely. In our role as problem solvers we will naturally come across highly sensitive data frequently. Care must be taken to ensure that we do not create additional vulnerabilities for our organization.

In our work, we have recognized two classes of sensitive information: company intellectual property and personal data. The first category applies to almost everything we touch as problem solvers, so the data as a whole, including the model source code, must be secured. It is not the subject of this book to cover the range of security measures that can and should be taken on any arbitrary collection of electronic data. I will assume for the moment that these "health and hygiene" measures are in place.

Creating that isolation between a human being and your need for their data and their meta-data is a process called *de-identification*. During data preparation, or perhaps the ETL process, we substitute the traceable information—a name or Social Security number or an address—with non-traceable information. So the name gets transformed into a coded ID, an address is aggregated into a zip code, and so on. The traceable source information remains in its secure original form.

Most problem solving does not require detailed traceable information on the human, so the transformation of the data in this way does not inhibit the problem solver.

Utilities

There are a number of software applications that aren't directly involved in the problem-solving workflow, yet assist that workflow in moving more efficiently from beginning to end.

Document Management

Numerous artifacts of the problem-solving process are generated continuously, and these must be managed carefully. Often a lot of time can pass between the agreement on a feature of the model, and the implementation of that feature in code, leaving you with a why-did-we-do-that-again feeling. In such cases, it is important to trace back to the reasoning, which is most likely contained in a document—an email from an SME, a batch of data handed to you, meeting notes.

The better document management systems (Evernote, Google Drive) allow you to place textual tags on documents for easy retrieval. An e-mail from Joe in accounting that explains how working capital is calculated might have the tags #Joe, #working_capital, and #accounting. Typing any one of these words (or something close) will get you to this document.

Most systems like this also create hyperlinks for each document. Hyperlinks come in very handy when you insert the links into positions in the qualitative model that relate to that link, making the qualitative model a versatile starting point for document searches.

Version Control

Multiple people constantly update project files. To maintain order over this activity, it is important to have a level of version control. For code, such systems are already well known: GitHub is a popular version control, collaboration, and archival system for code in virtually any language, allowing teams to interact with a code base, while making orderly and traceable (and reversible!) changes, even with multiple developers working on the same code.

For ordinary documents, applications like DropBox and Google Drive automatically register files on cloud-based storage, while keeping track of a rolling list of version history.

Project Management

Problem-solving projects are unique to many projects we deal with in corporate life. In simple terms, most projects are structured like this:

1. Draw up and agree on a specification.
2. Build the thing.
3. Test that it works.
4. Implement it across the organization.

The many subtasks are arranged onto a Gantt chart that is reviewed by the project team in a weekly status meeting. Sound familiar?

The challenge with problem solving is that there isn't a tidy specification; rather, the solution unfolds over time as the team learns more and more about the problem through various layers of the model. In short, *we don't know what we want until we see it*. Increasingly, software development as a whole is adopting this same approach, eschewing the highly detailed, rigid specification for a more incremental approach—build a little, share a little, build a little more, repeat until done. This is called the Agile methodology and has a formidable following within the commercial software development community. For good reason—the Agile method has produced some remarkable applications in a very short amount of time.

Model development for problem solving is similar in nature. If we are building a model that optimizes a bank's lending process to improve the quality of loans in the portfolio, we may start by creating a model that follows a single loan from end to end—a "day in the life" of the loan. That model is shared with the team—refinements made—then additional scope is added, say, all loans from one particular department in the bank, and so on until the entire scope is completed. Each cycle produces surprises and inspiration that can be driven into the next. The key to success is in designing each cycle—what the Agile community calls *sprints*—to be an effective and useful batch of features, while keeping the cycle time short (two weeks is a good guideline).

The Agile methodology is a rather formal set of processes and steps—one doesn't have to adopt the entire corpus of Agile to be a successful problem solver. At a minimum, simply break your development process into small development-then-review cycles and manage each cycle carefully and consistently, maintaining a working list of features along the way. Special software isn't required for project management here, but some teams do prefer project management apps that have an Agile methodology flavor to them, such as LeanKit, Trello, or Version One.

Chapter Summary

The technology that we use to solve problems has to be the best that it can be. Moreover, the toolset must be flexible enough to handle a wide range of problems that come our way, as it is crucial to match the nature of the problem to the features of the tool, to avoid harmful "tool bending" in unnatural ways. The four elements of workflow—design, data, computing, and visualization—must each have their complements of purpose-built applications and languages.

We have reached a milestone in our journey to problem-solving excellence by examining all of the ingredients of the technique—process, methods, data, visualization, and finally technology.

We are ready to "do" problem solving, and we are empowered.

CHAPTER 6

Using Your New Superpower

I remember my first interaction with a personal computer. These things were pretty new in 1981 during the Spring semester of my sophomore year in Engineering school. Our first assignment: write a program to draw a square on the screen. I probably fiddled around for a few days before I got the thing to work.

But when it did, something happened.

I stared at the screen for what seemed like hours. I did that—I made a square appear on the screen of a Northstar personal computer. Everything after that changed for me—my career, my understanding of the world around me, even my way of thinking. It was like waking up with X-ray vision or superhuman strength. Computer programming was my new superpower.

This probably seems rather puerile against today's landscape of computing everywhere, particularly to anyone under 40 who has never known life without ubiquitous personal computing. But at that time, programming on a personal computer was radically changing everything we knew—*and it was available to anyone who wanted in.*

Later, as a graduate student at Massachusetts Institute of Technology (MIT), most of my daily thoughts were around how to get a good enough job after graduation to pay off my huge student loans. However a few experiences there dramatically shaped my worldview on business problem solving—most notably my coursework in System Dynamics. There was something very different about this course compared to all of the other subjects. On the day of the first lecture the professor boldly claimed that he could clearly and simply explain such complex phenomena as the headline-grabbing failure of People Express Airlines or the scourge of drug abuse.

In the space of a 90-minute lecture, a business was deconstructed, reframed as a mathematical model, then reconstructed again, only in a form that allowed us to *simulate* a variety of possible outcomes for this company, bringing our insight about the strategy and structure of that company to a completely new plane.

There is no question that scientific approaches to complex problems provide extraordinary power, akin to a new pair of glasses. Details, shapes, and patterns that you hadn't noticed before all of a sudden appear with rich clarity. You see things that most people do not. Yet, as Ben Parker, Spiderman's uncle said, "With great power comes great responsibility." In other words, it is incumbent on us to use this power in appropriate, effective ways. That is what this chapter is all about. This is where the skills you have learned in the preceding chapters meet the human beings with whom you will interact to solve a problem.

What's the Problem?

It may sound a bit odd, but the first challenge in problem solving is finding the problems to solve, not because they aren't plentiful—they are quite literally all around you every day—but rather because the problems are often cloaked in the noise of everyday activity. Add to this the fact that human nature leans against talking about the problems we have—it is much more fun to talk about other subjects. Therefore, the problem solver is cast in a role of teasing tangible problems out of the beehive before the good work of solving can begin.

Believe it or not, there are good problems to solve and bad ones—problems that lend themselves well to the processes and methods we've just covered, and those that do not. So what constitutes a *good* problem?

There are several characteristics to look for. The presence of any two or more of these characteristics is an indicator that you likely have a good problem on your hands:

1. **The problem has lots of degrees of freedom to it**. A process inside a company is not working well to begin with, while the

company is thinking of an acquisition that would double the volume of transactions. Oh, and did we mention that marketing is introducing three new products this year that may or may not use the same process?

2. **The problem has a legacy.** Mary has been with the company for 45 years, and has always been in charge of solving problem X as it arises, not with data or science, mind you, but rather with her experience and knowledge accumulated over her career. By the way, Mary is retiring next month.

3. **The problem has never been solved after many tries.** It is an age-old challenge, and, oddly, some of our best minds have been working on variations of it for quite some time. Surely it just can't be done.

4. **The problem involves trade-offs.** The marketing team is pushing hard for an entry into a new geographic market. The CFO is pushing back, reasoning that this particular market is a credit risk. The two teams are actually arguing a trade-off between one financial metric at one extreme and another financial metric at the other. The Goldilocks Theorem suggests that somewhere "just right," in the middle is the right decision—but precisely where?

5. **The problem has a large price tag.** In some organizations, the difference between doing something well and doing something very well could be millions of dollars, justifying a search for gold using scientific methods.

6. **The problem has never been properly examined.** Certain systems in organizations, particularly important ones, "just happen" over time, with no one ever questioning how it works at a detailed level. The process of modeling a problem will have the byproduct of elaborating the problem systematically and objectively.

7. **The problem today is solved 100 percent manually.** An army of humans with their disparate spreadsheets works hard on the problem and somehow arrives at a solution. Rinse and repeat next month.

Does any of this sound familiar? I know that I have heard these markers many times in my 30 years of solving problems, and they provide me instant clues about the alignment of the techniques we have discussed with the problem at hand.

Getting Started

Typically there are three elements to bring together at the onset of problem solving: the people, the problem, and the technology.

People

When we talk about people, we are really talking about roles. In some cases, multiple roles may be served by more than one person, yet each role is distinctly mapped to a certain set of tasks.

The *executive sponsor* ensures that the problem and its solution are recognized across the company, is properly funded, and serves as a template for future problem solving.

A *business agent* is the benefactor of the solution, and consequently owns the original problem (the "victim"). While this person is part of the company, we refer to her as the client or the customer.

SMEs provide the logic and terminology of the problem, and are deeply involved in the validation of the resulting solution.

The *solver team* works the problem through the process of solving the problem and reports on progress. They are responsible for the solution as well as the generation and the archiving of the artifacts of the problem-solving process. Inside the team you will have people with programming, data management, and math skills. The solvers should be knowledgeable about the domain of the problem, but not so much so that they are classed as SMEs. *A good dose of isolation from the subject matter is a good thing*, as it keeps the teams asking naive questions that a deeply entrenched SME might gloss over.

Project managers attend to schedules for delivery and orchestrate the Agile activities to incrementally build out the solution.

Problem

At the outset, the problem you are looking at is typically not well formed—it might even be a topic that has been verbally discussed around the company but never articulated, or perhaps even a blend of multiple problems that seem related. In the rare case that the problem is clear, we proceed with the hypothesis stage, as discussed in chapter 1. In the more common case where the problem is a degree or two unclear, we start with a whiteboard session.

The whiteboard session, as the name implies, is an informal discussion among a small group of people knowledgeable about the problem. Here the problem solver uses his or her judgment to tease out the problem, watching carefully for terminology that defines it correctly. Sessions are typically timeboxed at a couple of hours, with perhaps a handful of follow-on one-to-one sessions with particular individuals for clarification and detail.

There is no particular format that one should rigidly follow when conducting a whiteboard session. Rather it involves "thinking out loud" as you ask questions of the SMEs and build on their answers. Some of the best whiteboard sessions I have personally led have been messy and awkward, leaving most of the participants feeling like it was a rambling, chaotic conversation. Rarely does the human mind think linearly when confronted with a brand new problem to think about—noise and smoke are a natural consequence. These kinds of sessions are often much better than a formal (meaning tense) Q&A meeting.

The end result of a whiteboard session should be a graphic interlaced judiciously with text annotations, usually built within a day or two of the conclusion of the session (see example shown in Figure 6.1). The focus of the graphic should be the problem, not the solution, although it is acceptable to vaguely hint at a solution at this stage. Each problem should have its own graphic if there is more than one emerging from the session.

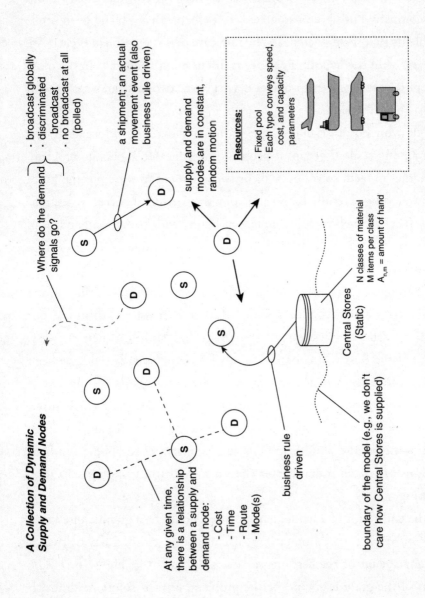

Figure 6.1 Typical output from a whiteboard session. This particular problem involved the deconstruction of a supply chain for a global manufacturer

Technology

Part of getting started is staging the technical tools in advance of their use. We want to avoid getting a nice detailed description of a problem only to have to wait a few weeks until the technology is ready to use. Yet prestaging technology is a tricky challenge—we do not know with 100 percent confidence which tools might apply. Certainty is always a luxury in problem solving. You will simply have to make good guesses as to which technologies are likely to be useful given the vague nature of the problem at the outset.

It is also important to avoid the "let's go gather data" mindset. We have seen this attitude in a number of engagements in our practice: a call to gather all of the data we might need down the road. This can be a painful and tedious process, and in the worst case can even kill a project by sapping its momentum. It also leads to a lot of wasted effort in collecting data that isn't actually needed for the solution. Best practice is to let the model *show* you what data is needed and *then* collect accordingly.

Working with Subject Matter Experts

This book is about the application of science to business problems, but there is a surprising amount of art that goes into doing it well. One of the highest forms of art is the interaction between the problem solver and the SMEs—a case study in human psychology.

Why? Because humans unintentionally lie. Their egos cause them to discuss things they are personally proud of, as the subject matter is their lifelong profession. They fear exposing their knowledge to outsiders, or perhaps feel that those outside of their expertise will not understand. In short, they are human—imperfect and at times irrational. And you, the solver, have to bend their will in your direction.

There is a particular dynamic at play when you have more than one SME of the same type in the room. They may be answering your question, but at the top of their mind is how they look in front of their peers, and this colors their responses. So while it is good to do the first few kick-off sessions in a group, it is important to move on quickly to one-on-one sessions in order to get the full story.

When interacting with an SME, it is best to start with very broad questions like "How does ___ work?" or "Walk me through how ___ unfolds across the day." This gives the SME the freedom to cover topics that you didn't think about asking. The vast majority of SMEs need very little prompting to spur a reaction. You will have more of a challenge cutting off discussion than getting it started.

As they speak, start tracking on a line of reasoning and keep them focused on that. I tell my SMEs in advance that I will be interrupting them frequently and not to take offense at that. It is important to draw a picture as they speak; to translate their spoken prose into a graphical mirror of the system, in whatever form suits. Words are crucial—every organization has a unique body of language, often loaded with acronyms—and the problem solver must quickly master this language and incorporate it into the design documents for them to be effectively communicated. However, be prepared for words in one department to take on a whole different meaning in another! Organizations are often surprised how language dialects emerge among different factions.

Once you have followed your line of reasoning, cut off discussion and move on to the next topic. This is difficult, because the SME will want to discuss the subject to death with every possible variant of how things work. There is a reason that TED Talks, whether it is Bono or Billy Graham—are *always* limited to 18 minutes.

Verboseness is in direct conflict with the problem solver's mission of capturing a majority of the information, but leaving the last 20 percent for later refinement. There is definitely a Pareto distribution at work here. Be careful to note when the incremental discussion is not generating a proportional level of new information. It helps to steer SMEs to talking about the "normal" way things unfold in the system and leave the exceptions to a later discussion once the normal system has been vetted.

Within days show the SME the picture you have drawn of the conversation. More than likely she will say, "It's roughly right, but this part over here needs a change." Make the refinements and check back as many cycles as needed until the SME agrees that your diagram represents the system at hand accurately. Keep in mind that SMEs often feel uncomfortable that the last ten years of their career can be summed up in a one-page diagram.

The combined corpus of diagrams will now comprise the hypothesis and qualitative models that we introduced in chapter 1. Depending on the organization, it can be helpful to link the SME contributor to regions of the diagram using the layering feature we mentioned in chapter 5.

Showing a comprehensive qualitative model that sums the collective knowledge of the organization back to the whole project team is one of the most rewarding things you can do as a problem solver. I have had plenty of substantial "Ah ha" moments coming out of the qualitative model's revelation.

Cross-Collaboration

Crafting a good qualitative model of a particular problem does something subtle—it strips away the parochial layers of industry and company to illustrate the fundamental aspects of the problem. Doing this over and over across a lot of problems allows us to think more broadly about the problem at hand, in particular, how other industries or companies might have solved a similar kind of problem. Adapting ideas from one industry or situation into another is called cross-collaboration, and problem solvers are uniquely positioned to innovate in this way.

The best problem solvers are "students" of problems—wherever they may lie. Make a practice of looking outside your industry at organizations that have grappled with particular problems. You will surprise yourself with your acumen at spotting common approaches and expressing them graphically, particularly if you practice it regularly. Cross-collaboration is one of the most underutilized sources of innovation today, yet is easily within our grasp.

Baby Steps

With the design stage of the project completed, you now move into the development of the quantitative model, which is often a replica of the system you have described with the qualitative model. That means writing the code for the model, getting it to a state where it is generating results from the data. In chapter 5, we introduced the idea of the Agile methodology as an organized means of building the model up in small steps with frequent reviews, as opposed to building it all at once over a longer period with a review at the end.

What is a good small step to start with? I recommend using a step that includes the whole system, but using a fraction of the data. So, for example, if you are creating a corporate sales forecasting model for a retailer, start by forecasting just one store, or perhaps sales from just one class of customer, or one product category. Most systems have natural increments to them—use those as your boundaries and pretend, for the moment, that this little fraction of the organization is the only thing that exists. Then, in a second step, scale to the next increment, and the next.

The model itself might consist of rules, transforms, equations, feedback loops, and/or method algorithms of the type described in chapter 2. In any case, the qualitative model and the hypothesis collectively form the guide for the structure of the model that will answer the hypothesis question.

A former professor of mine used to say, "Always have a working model." It is one of the best pieces of advice I have ever received. What he meant was to quickly build a model that runs, without error, on some fraction of the data. It will be incomplete, to be sure, but it will be enough of the final system for SMEs and others on the project team to envision how it will look once completed. They will be actively engaged with the model, advising you much more effectively with the model in front of them, on changes and features to add. If on the other hand you insist on the model getting to a 90 percent completion before you show it to anyone, you will have lost momentum, and more than likely the team may have forgotten the problem this model was trying to solve!

The Agile methodology comes with all sorts of ceremony and rules. You are not required to adopt every facet of the Agile religion in order to be successful. However, at minimum you should engage the following practices:

1. *Always maintain a running list of the total tasks to be done.* Of particular note are the tasks that map directly to a feature in the model such as "Change the calculation of consumer sentiment to incorporate past purchases." In our company we use Evernote to track all of our task lists.

2. *Each development step is a defined list of tasks.* Pick a time window— no more than a few weeks—and make a separate list of the tasks from the master list that will be accomplished in that time window.

3. *Frequent reviews.* Review the model at the end of every development step. Run it for the project team to show them how it works. Repetition breeds familiarity, and familiarity breeds confidence. Avoid making these reviews hour-long affairs—show the model in ten minutes or less, and only extend it if there are questions and comments to be discussed. Best practice is to maintain the model in some location, say at a particular uniform resource locator (URL), so that anyone in the project team can get to the model at any time.

Bias

Let me tell you a story about bias in problem solving. I was once asked by a company to model a potential merger between that company and another. "Wall Street doesn't understand our logic," a Sr. VP told me. "So we need a model to express the reasoning of the merger so that they get our long-term strategy with the combined organizations."

"Ah, ok," I said, "so I will model the merger, and if the numbers look right, you will proceed with the merger and present the rationale to the analysts using the model."

"Well, not exactly," the VP explained, "the CEOs already agreed to the merger on the golf course, and your model will tell us if we made the right decision."

Not exactly what I wanted to hear. I didn't want to be put in a situation where a particular outcome was desired from the model—a certain recipe for bias that had my moral compass spinning. Only after weeks of assurances from their senior staff that they would not bias the data or the process of modeling did I agree to take on the assignment. Oddly, in the end the financial case for the merger was so strong that bias would not likely have altered the model outcome much, but the lesson from that experience was clear—model bias is an ever-present danger to problem solvers, even those with the best of intentions.

To distinguish between legitimate judgment and opinion and bias is a particular challenge. Even so, there are a few guidelines you can use to prevent bias from creeping into your models.

- **Which problem are you trying to solve?** Bias can begin at the beginning—showing up in your selection of the problem to solve. The question you should ask yourself is, "Is this is the right problem, or am I narrowing or broadening the problem deliberately to get an outcome I want?"

- **Make assumptions transparent and changeable**. Bias can arise in the assumptions that underlie numerical parameters that form inputs to your models. I recall a heated debate in an oil company about whether the "ChanceOfSuccess" parameter in a new round of oil wells was to be 0.30 or 0.35. In the end we settled the debate by trying every possible CoS value in our model runs from 0 to 1.0 in increments of 0.05.

- **Avoid tuning.** Sometimes people will try to "tune" the model to a certain singular outcome by playing with the input parameters until that outcome is reached, then freeze that version of the model to present to others as "final." It is much better to run the model across ranges of inputs and present the distribution of outcomes. Always be skeptical of single-value model runs.

Model Validation

You have built a model that runs and generates the kinds of the results that look sensible. It works. Congratulations. You have one last step before proceeding to live experimentation with the model, and that is validation.

Validation involves the comprehensive vetting of the model with the SMEs in a way that confirms that the model results are correct. The stamp of approval from the organization's smartest people will ensure that the model's underlying logic will not be needlessly questioned, and that we can make decisions inspired by the model's output with confidence.

There are two classes of questions to answer in the validation process:

Is the Model Calculating the Results Correctly According to How I Have Coded It?

Here we assume that the blueprint is correct. The question is, does the math match the blueprint? Bugs can creep into the code, causing a sensible input to generate an incorrect output.

Is the Model Using the Right Logic?

Assuming we pass the test in question #1—we have determined that our model is correctly performing the logic calculations—the next question is whether our logic is correct in the first place. There could have been an error in the problem solver's translation of the SME's instructions, or, it could even be an error by the SME. In either case, a failure here means that you are correctly calculating an incorrect piece of logic.

Validation in these two domains requires very different approaches. In step 1, the problem solver can largely carry out the validation herself, setting up parallel "by hand" calculations in a spreadsheet and comparing the results there to the model's outputs using the same data.

In step 2, SMEs are drafted to assist. We most often start with a sample set of inputs, while the expected outputs are hidden from the problem solver—a so-called single-blind test. When model results are subsequently compared to the expected results, only one of two outcomes is possible—either the results are in the range of the expected or the results are uncomfortably outside of that range. In the former case, we continue with more samples until we are convinced that the model is producing sensible results even when we mix up the outputs. In the latter case, it is important to recognize that failing the sense check does not in any way mean that the model is wrong—it is simply generating a counterintuitive result. The model could very well be correct, and some of the most interesting and valuable debates occur when explaining how the model arrived at these surprising results. Model failure can actually lead to a huge project success.

Assuming we have the latter case or any single failure in the former, the next logical step is to conduct a forensics session with the model.

The Forensics Session

As the name suggests, a forensics session involves placing the model on the operating table and cutting into it in strategic places to find evidence of a failure. Most models consist of chains of transformations of data until the final result is realized, so examining each transform bit by bit is a healthy exercise for understanding where the failures lie.[1]

The software analogue of an operating table is the test bench. These are all highly language-specific, but the function is the same—take code fragments and run them in isolation to determine whether the transform is correctly carried out. Most bugs that we see occur somewhere in the sequence, and then the failure cascades forward, through to the end result. Therefore, in most situations, starting with the first transform and moving through the remaining ones in execution sequence makes a lot of sense.

SME involvement at this stage is not required, but in my experience this can be highly valuable. As the SMEs begin to see precisely how the calculations are performed internally, a light usually comes on and they begin to grasp how the model is implementing their formerly mental logic. This approach is a subtle way to bring the SMEs on side, which can pay dividends down the road.

Unit Testing

You have fully validated the model with your SMEs as partners. It was time consuming and at times painful, but now you have a fully validated model. Hooray!

Someone suggests a small feature change. You make the change, and...wait, does that mean I have to go through that whole validation process all over again? Thankfully, no. Unit testing comes to your rescue, as we described generally in chapter 5. Unit testing is the name for a prebuilt series of tests of certain aspects of your code. It can be thought of in this way: "If I give my model X as an input, I expect to get Y as an output." Unit tests are created over the course of the development process and are usually packaged together to run in sequence. A test that consists of eight units should run all eight and pass all eight. Should any given test fail, that test will guide you to the general location of the failure.

Unit tests don't have to describe a specific result with the data. An input of five into the model to get an expected result of ten is very specific. A good unit test framework allows you to test for symbolic results, such as, "If I put in a list of six numbers, I should get a list of fifteen numbers out, all real values in the range of 0 to 1."

Now back to our validated example. If you have set up unit tests and then validated the model on a version that has passed all of the unit tests, with few exceptions a change to that model that passes all unit tests will not require revalidation. Most ordinary bugs will not require revalidation either—only substantial changes to the logic.

The Role of Visualization in Validation

I recall an experience of running a model for a room full of SMEs. They all worked for an airline, and we were analyzing a model that related to the airline's performance across its route network. The visualization was literally an animation of airplanes darting across a map of the United States.

"Hey, I see something wrong here," said an operations specialist in the back of the room. "That flight from Omaha to Amarillo. We canceled that last month." Sure enough, he was right. It turns out that we were using a route schedule that was slightly out of date—some modifications to the schedule had happened since our last data upload.

We had a bug in our model—what we refer to as a data bug, because while the logic of the model was correct, we fed it the wrong information. Think about what just happened—this SME was watching the visualization, and out of all of the hundreds of segments flown, he spotted one in particular that led us to discover the source of the bug. What if he had been looking at a spreadsheet with a dizzying array of numbers flicking back and forth? It is unlikely he would have spotted this at all. It was the visualization that not only made it real to him but also invited him into the validation process on peer level.

This story is important because it highlights an often overlooked tool in the validation arsenal: the visualization itself. Human brains are wonderful pattern recognizers, and visualization bridges the gap between the model and the human very effectively.

Running Experiments

Now comes the fun part—running experiments using your freshly validated model. At its simplest level, an experiment is simply a result paired with the set of inputs that led to that result. Best practice suggests performing experiments in two arenas: interactive and offline.

The model interface should contain user controls like checkboxes, drop down selectors, sliders, radio buttons, and the like situated on the left-hand side of the page. The results—graphs, animations, tables—are shown on the right-hand side. As you change the inputs by operating the controls, you directly see the impact that has on the results. This allows your audience to see, in a very direct and visceral way, how the model works and, more importantly, how the real system will behave under certain conditions (see an example in Figure 6.2). It also shows the audience which of these inputs is more impactful to the outcome, often referred to as sensitivity analysis. If your audience is engaged, they may ask questions in real time, which can be answered by the model. "What would happen if you ___?" The interactive style of experimentation is an important step toward communicating solutions and building confidence in the model.

Before experimentation with SMEs and others outside the solver team takes place, it is wise to conduct a final check of the model and its interface against the hypothesis that you created weeks or months earlier. Does the model answer the hypothesis question through experimentation?

Not all experiments can be done interactively. Some require time to set up, run, and document the results. You will not want your interactive audience to wait more than a few minutes for a result (nor will they). In these cases, you should engage in experiments away from the audience and present the collective results when done. Given that most people will want to see a wide range of results, offline experimentation usually involves running every possible state of the system, or at least a feasible range of states. A helpful template for offline experiments is the strategy matrix, mentioned in previous chapters. A strategy matrix is a table of results in which the rows represent various settings of an input, and the columns represent various settings of another input. The cells at the intersection are the results given the two input settings.

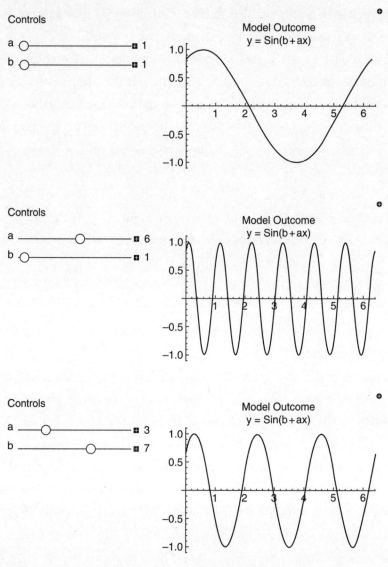

Figure 6.2 A very simple model with interactivity (built using *Mathematica*)

More than two inputs mean more than one strategy matrix—one for each setting of the third input, and so on. An additional input may mean that each cell in the matrix is split into multiple views. The idea is to home in on the solution by showing a pattern in the model's results. This rarely calls for every possible input to be incorporated into the matrix.

Choose the two or more input sets that are the most impactful for inclusion into the row/column arrangement. You can also supplement the strategy matrix by selecting a single output metric and plotting it across a range of inputs.

Case Study in Experimentation: The Elusive Drug Pipeline

We had spent months perfecting a model of a drug pipeline for a major pharmaceutical manufacturer. When we finally made it through rounds of validation, we were ready to start experimenting. It turns out that this company had struggled with its development pipeline for years, spending extraordinary amounts of money but with few successful drugs coming out at the end. This was a very well-managed company with experienced, talented people in charge. What went wrong?

Our first few simulation runs didn't reveal anything special. Put compounds in one end, a few billion dollars to move them through, get a tiny fraction of successful drugs out. While the model mimicked the real system quite well, it didn't give us a wealth of insight as to why it was performing so poorly.

By complete accident (it was actually a bug in the code), we killed one of the major drug programs early in the cycle. The financials *improved.* "This can't be right," we thought... "killing that particular program? It was one of the more successful ones!" It turns out that this was a surprisingly good reflection of the real world at this firm. Certain programs were latched onto by the medical sponsors, who had an almost "emotional" attachment to continuing the good fight to keep the program alive in spite of setbacks. The more charismatic and reputable the sponsor, the less likely the program would be killed.

As we did more checking, it turns out that the model, as it was programmed to do, moved that money to a series of other smaller programs whose collective success exceeded the bigger program. The math was correct.

That got us thinking…what if we configured the model to be much more aggressive in killing promising but weaker development programs early in the cycle, before investment rates increased? That experiment failed miserably…far too few programs made it all the way through. What if we backed off that aggressiveness just a bit? Bingo…we found a sweet spot where overall value jumped severalfold.

The ensuing insight from several runs of the model sparked a significant change in the company strategy—one in which programs were ruthlessly but intelligently killed early to make way for more promising developments. Mathematical markers were developed to make the "kill zone" in the pipeline more apparent and accurate.

Experimentation requires patience and reflection…the answer doesn't just tumble out of the model on day one. It is more the norm than the exception to work with a model over and over until the transformation is well understood.

Users

Problem solvers don't often think of themselves as software vendors. They see themselves as solving a problem, and software helps the process. However, once you put a model out into a space where people other than yourself are using your model, you become an erstwhile software vendor for the organization. And what most good software vendors do is think about their users.

Who is your user? The immediate image that comes to mind is the person who runs the model. Check a few boxes, slide some sliders, click run, get a result—these are the folks your solution was designed for. Fair enough, but there is another class of user you may have overlooked—the *super* user. A super user has the power not only to use the model but also to change the underlying data that feeds the model. If that person isn't you, consideration must be given to how easily the super user can perform her job. Are the data tables nicely aligned and well documented? How do model errors show up?

Give some thought to the care and handling of the whole model and develop a set of guidelines for super users to follow. Doing so will ensure that the model continues to build confidence across the organization.

Solution to Execution

A successful solution rarely stands still. The problem's owner will spring into action and incorporate the solution into the real-world system right away. It is now a year later. Did the solution actually work in practice?

Our goal as problem solvers is to ensure that the real-world problem is solved, not just on paper but also in tangible use. Therefore, a periodic evaluation of the solution as it migrates into the real world is just as much a part of the solution as is the development of the model that preceded it.

It is unrealistic to think that the solution will work as perfectly and precisely as it did in the controlled conditions of the virtual laboratory. The noise of the real world creates deviations. This does not mean the model isn't useful, but it does require that we explain any substantial deviations between real-world performance and the model's performance. Political pollsters do this all the time—they compare how their model predicted the election outcome against what actually happened, and then tune the model to pick up anything it had missed. It works. In case you hadn't noticed, election models have grown to become astonishingly accurate in the last five US presidential election cycles.

Yet another way we can strengthen the relationship between the solution and the real world is to cast the model forward in the form of a dashboard. Note that the user interface to the model contained a visualization of the results on the right-hand side panel. This might have been expressed in the form of a set of plots, individual metrics on a dial, and so forth. The code to create that right-hand representation could be lifted out and reimplemented as a dashboard. Instead of relying on model feeds, however, the dashboard is taking in real-world metrics in real time. This facilitates a model-to-actual comparison and ensures that the same metrics we diligently watched in the laboratory are also observed in the real world as the system goes about its daily duties.

Data as Art/Art as Data

Walk through any modern office these days and you are likely to see some pretty snazzy artwork adorning the walls. That makes for a nice-looking atmosphere, but as the art never changes, after a while most everyone ignores the images.

For those organizations seeking to instill a culture of data and analytical curiosity into the organization, an alternative to the artwork is a series of digital monitors attached to a server. The server is programmed to display a sequence of continuously updating dashboards fed by real-time information. The displays are mesmerizing, particularly when they show metrics vital to the business. Dynamic visual artifacts might even spark a rigorous hallway debate that leads to an important finding.

In some cases, the code of the model can be incorporated into the production IT systems to carry out the work of the system that governs the real-world function. For example, if you create a model of a supply chain, parts of the model can run the logic of the dispatching function. If you create a model of a bank, part of the model can be incorporated into the routing logic for transactions. Importing logic from models to production IT systems is an often overlooked source of substantial value from problem solving.

From Model Experiment to Model Immersion:
Management Flight Simulators

In some cases, it isn't enough just to come up with a solution. It isn't enough to communicate the solution across the organization. Rather, in these cases, it is important to *evangelize* the solution everywhere—to hold the solution up as an opportunity to teach a broad swath of people the key principles that underlie the system. True evangelism requires the use of a management flight simulator (MFS).

You may have seen the huge elaborate machines that airlines use to train pilots. Inside a cocoon-like pod sits an exact replica of an airplane's cockpit. The pilot climbs in, starts the engines, and flies through a series of scenarios built into the simulator's logic. The test might include an engine failure or a bird strike, and the pilot is expected to react accordingly in order to safely navigate the plane. Even the most senior pilots are required to spend time on the simulator.

One of the most exciting things about solving problems in the way that I describe in this book is that these practices lend themselves well to the straightforward extension of models into MFSs—simulation models that work much like their airline counterparts—but instead of flying an airplane we are flying (managing) an organization. Originally developed at MIT, management flight simulators have become a fixture at leading business schools for teaching strategy.

Here's how MFSs work: you've just spent considerable time and resources building a model of an organization, or at least some significant part of that organization. You have inputs on the left-hand panel and results on the right. It doesn't require a great deal of code to turn that interface into a game-like use case, in which the user can now act as the leader of the organization, deciding on a strategy, mapping that onto some input settings, then clicking "Run," and running, say, a one-year implication of that strategy. The decision/run cycle is repeated across several years, emulating the management of an organization over a long period of time.

In my years of doing this work, I have seen successful applications of MFSs across the spectrum, from the simple game playing on a desktop computer by curious individuals, to elaborate off-site events with competitive teams, formal debriefs, and multiple rounds of game play. But in each the result was the same—people came away from this experience with a very deep and profound sense of how the system worked, and how it works differently with the new solution in place.

The use of the MFS concept in an organization underscores a particular philosophy of corporate strategy that involves *practice*.

It's hard to think of any professional sport that doesn't involve hours and hours of practice. And not just practice but also the coaching during and the debriefs afterward are a huge part of the preparation for the big game. In effect, the drills emulate the real competition, and certain drills are designed very carefully to address specific parts of the tapestry of skills needed over the course of the contest.

Do we practice in business? Hardly ever. Think about it: when was the last time you "practiced" the launch of a new product line, the fulfillment of a big customer order, or even the acquisition of a new firm? In business, we tend to do strategic work head-on, with little to no formal preparation—we "dive right in."

Now ask yourself how many times you have come to the end of one of these enterprise projects and questioned, "Gee, if I had known it would have gone this way, I would have done something very different." Avoidable rookie mistakes are often the anecdotes that become the highlight of water cooler conversations.

But how do we practice in business? These big efforts don't come along very often, so how could we possibly prepare for something like that?

By creating realistic MFSs of the company, we can not only test certain policy decisions but we can also walk through—no, actually *live through*—these strategies as they unfold. Moreover, our best and brightest talent (current and retired) can anchor the simulated exercises as coaches, guiding us through a logical set of decisions. The point is that you are practicing for the day when these insights and skills will be brought to bear on real problems inside the real company. Wouldn't you rather meet that challenge having done a variant of it hundreds of times before?

Being a Good Client

Of the many people who read this book, some will not be problem solvers but rather problem owners. Others are developing the solution on your behalf. You are the *client*. What many clients don't realize is that their role in the solution is not a passive one. Becoming a "good" client will result in a good solution. The converse is true as well.

Here are some guidelines for good clients:

1. **Be careful what you ask for**. Many clients insist on a high degree of realism in models, at times an inappropriate level of realism. This in turn causes the problem solvers to build useless detail into the model. Become comfortable with the idea that this model is an abstraction of the real-world system, and deviations from that are OK, in fact, desirable. You are looking for insight from the model, not a precise prediction. The hypothesis is a useful guide as to how much realism is needed just to solve the problem.

2. **Incorporate baby step thinking into the development process**. Clients aren't typically shown a model or any piece of software until it is almost complete. But that isn't the way models should be built; rather, it should be brick by brick through an agile set of cycles. Therefore, it isn't so important that any one version of the model be absolutely correct. It is far more important that the *trend* of the development is getting closer and closer to the solution over time.

3. **Welcome naive questions**. Problem solvers who are not conversant in the system at hand will ask questions that industry veterans will dismiss as naive. Don't let this happen. Often the naive questions can lead to investigations of long-held beliefs in the industry that are no longer valid. Naiveté is healthy—encourage more of it and not less.

Repurposing Models

One of the most gratifying things to observe in action is the inspiration that problem solving can instill in a group of talented people. Creating a model to solve a problem often spurs creative thinkers to devise other ways to use that model.

Years ago, I built a model to optimize a supply chain. Our goal was to wring unnecessary costs out of the system by intelligently constructing land and sea routes for the cargoes. The model worked quite well and became a permanent fixture of the company's operations.

One of the young engineers who worked with me to build the model moved on to a completely separate project to look at the organization's response to severe storms, as operations are significantly disrupted in such cases, creating safety risks to personnel and millions of dollars in lost revenue. "Hey," he thought, "I wonder if that supply chain model could show us the impact of severe weather events?" Thus, the severe storm model was born, or perhaps a better word would be "cloned." Ninety percent of the severe storm model was already in the supply chain model. The company used it to stress test their systems under dozens of weather scenarios and make surgical changes to operations to ensure business continuity and the safety of its personnel even in these extreme cases.

Treat your models as prized assets to be used anywhere. Make a detailed list of all of the models that exist in the organization, large and small, and illustrate the core underlying functions that live within each. A periodic review of this asset portfolio against the "problems of the day" will likely inspire reasoned thinking about how to leverage the existing assets to quickly build new solutions.

Chapter Summary

The ability to solve a problem through the mechanism of a computer model is like having a superpower. Like any superpower, it must be directed to perform the most good.

When models meet people, interesting things happen. This chapter offered several guidelines for making that interaction valuable. Done well, problem solving can transform an institution's performance using nothing more than the collective wisdom already inside the four walls.

Congratulations on finding your new superpower. But what if you joined forces with others who had similar but distinct superpowers? Can you imagine what could be done with a *team* of like-minded superheroes?

Let's go build that team.

CHAPTER 7

Setting the Stage: The Making of a Great Problem-Solving Team

Building teams within organizations begins with leadership. The following is a paraphrased conversation I had with a CEO many years ago, just after we had completed a very complex pricing model for his industrial products company:

CEO: "Thanks for coming to see me, George."

George: "Thank you for inviting me. I'll have to admit that I am a little nervous here. Is there something wrong with the model we built for you?"

CEO: "That is just what I wanted to talk about. No, there's nothing wrong with the model. I've been following its progress...It has really helped us develop some insights, and it solved a particularly important problem for us. It was just what we needed."

George: "Wow, that is good to hear."

CEO: "But..." (long pause)

George: "Yes, go on..."

CEO: "...the insights from running the model gave me a new way of thinking about how our company should operate. We asked you to streamline our pricing process and you did, and we are happy about that. But it also left me a bit unsettled...why can't our company build models to solve problems in the way that you did? On any given day, we have dozens of problems to solve that are of the same importance as the one that you worked on. How do I channel my own talent here to do that?"

George: "My own observation of your company is that everyone here is directed to one thing: fighting fires. They deal with the back end of the problems. The 'problem' with that is that they do it so well with sweat and long hours that the company continues to prosper in spite of itself. People are rewarded here for doing a good job at firefighting, and are barely recognized for putting in smoke detectors."

CEO: "I don't disagree. But where does that leave us?"

George: "Build a team...a team that is geared specifically to the practice of problem solving. The members of this team will likely come from outside the industry."

CEO: "A bunch of brainy prima donnas with no experience in our industry? That wouldn't work well in our culture."

George: "It doesn't have to go down that way. There are several successful examples out there, and there are a few tips and tricks to pulling it off that we can discuss."

CEO: "If this works, it would be an amazing capability for our company, a legacy I can leave to my successor. If it fails, it will be personally embarrassing to me and a poor reflection on my leadership here. The optics on this will be intense."

George: "It's a calculated risk, to be sure. But consider the tailwind you have here. You've got exceptionally talented people. You have a technology team that is eager to support activity that directly impacts the business. You have the investment capital to do it right. The board's strategic imperatives map precisely to the goals of a problem-solving team."

CEO: "Yeah, fine. But I still feel like I am making a leap of faith here."

George: "It is."

(another long pause)

CEO: "Alright, then. We had better get started."

He did move ahead with the creation of a problem-solving team, and was in fact very successful with it. When he retired three years later, the team had grown to more than a dozen members, and the company was a leader in its industry that was head and shoulders above other companies, in part because of the incredible work that was done by this roving team.

That process was not smooth sailing, and in fact prior to that success there were a series of agonizing mistakes that we all made in crafting a problem-solving capability for the company. We hired the wrong people, used the wrong tools, and tackled the wrong problems. In short, we made every mistake one could make in our attempt to *institutionalize* the act of problem solving. We did get two things right, however. First, the CEO was steadfast in building the capability in spite of the hiccups. Second, we committed to learning from each mistake by conducting painfully frank evaluations of what went wrong.

There is keen interest these days in building problem-solving teams not unlike the characters in Michael Lewis' widely acclaimed book *Moneyball*,[1] maniacally poring over every baseball metric to find a pattern to exploit. Done well, the transformation in an organization can be just as dramatic as it was for the Oakland Athletics baseball team. In this chapter, we will summarize what it takes to build truly great problem-solving teams. We will further discuss how to position those teams for success by crafting proper roles for their work. This guidance is just as relevant for team members, their collaborators, and their end customers, as well as for the leadership.

Evolving a Capability

I have seen three successful models of problem-solving capability arise in organizations: grass-roots, rover, and accordion. These are by no means the only models from which to choose, but they do represent useful starting points.

In the grass-roots model, the organization lays down a set of bedrock principles, not dissimilar to the concepts we have discussed up to now, creates a technical environment as shown in chapter 5, and constructs a means to highlight and communicate local successes. Other groups get the message and begin to adopt the principles as well. Soon a social norm in the company is created where the problem-solving practices are engraved in the culture. It is "the way we do things around here."

With the rover model, a dedicated team (perhaps even a team of one) tackles some of the most challenging and sweeping problems, constantly trolling the organization for new ones to identify and solve. As they work, they evangelize the practice of problem solving among others.

Finally, with the accordion model, the organization chooses to focus on core operations and rely on an outside team to perform the problem-solving function. That team grows and shrinks (sometimes to zero) over the course of many projects as needed to fit the workload of the moment. Over time, the outside team works as an extension of the organization, almost indistinguishable from the staff.

Any of these models or combinations thereof can be made to work, but the end goal is the same: to create a durable problem-solving culture inside the company (as opposed to a problem-*handling* culture).

The grass-roots model is particularly challenging to start and manage, as it relies on change occurring throughout the organization organically, without a champion leading the way. Still, some organizations are infused with eager, talented people in positions of influence who can pull off the institutional practice of problem solving.

If yours is like most organizations, however, a constant active presence is needed over a long time period to effect the change from the status quo to a problem-solving company. In this case, the rover and accordion models in particular can be most effective.

Leadership

Usually the rover teams start as a team of one—the person initially brought in to start the effort stays on to lead the team as is grows. That puts extra pressure on you in choosing the first person. Here are some characteristics to look for in that interview:

1. **Most, if not all, of career spent outside of the industry of the organization**. It is nice to have someone conversant about the industry, but don't follow the norm of recruiting someone with

significant experience inside it. You are looking for an individual who will ask the naive questions and give a fresh perspective on problems.

2. **A track record of versatility.** A person who has made a successful, significant leap from one industry to another or from one function to another shows that they have mastered "quick learning."

3. **Programming.** Even if it is far back in the candidate's history, work in a computer programming capacity sets the stage for the kind of systemic thinking that will be vital in the role, not to mention a useful hands-on grounding in technology.

4. **Has an instinct to draw.** When asked about a particular project or how they solved some problem, is their first tendency to rush to a whiteboard and start making pictures? Are the pictures clear and simple to understand?

5. **Has worked with or managed smart creatives.**[2] Hyper-smart, creative people are a unique challenge to manage. Is there evidence in the candidate's background that they are a smart creative themselves or have successfully led a team of them?

6. **Is OK with getting hands dirty.** Team members respect a leader who is on their same level technically, one who can in theory jump right into a project and write code alongside them. The best among leaders actually assign themselves occasional duties in projects to keep their technical skills sharp.

The Team

At some stage of maturity, it will be time to add members to the team of one. What kinds of people do we look for? This is one of the most frequent questions I get in the work that I do with organizations.

Most business people assume that problem solving is primarily about the deep mathematical methods that we discussed in chapter 2. That is an important part of the equation, but as we get down into the skill set that drives success, we find that the *programming* side of problem solving is the most important skill to master at the outset. Given a choice between a very good mathematician who is "just ok" at programming versus a programmer who had basic math courses, I would pick the programmer every time.

An ideal candidate is one who comes from a completely different industry or discipline, yet can explain the work that she does, understandably, in a couple of simple diagrams. This is the mark of a person who will adapt well to an entirely new industry, something we call "end to end" thinking. These folks also tend to be more collaborative in nature.

One thing to avoid in interviews of team members is this common practice of introducing a sample problem and asking the candidate to solve it in a few minutes' time. While that may reveal thought processes, it is an assessment of how well the candidate comes to snap judgments about the problem, which in my book is a negative rather than a positive attribute (oddly, major consulting firms find the ability to make snap judgments highly attractive).

For my money I do not want candidates who rattle off solutions to problems based on five minutes of thinking. A better alternative is to give the candidate a sample problem to take home and to bring back no sooner than 48 hours with an approach to the problem.

"What if the candidate cheats?" I hear this all the time. "She will call up her smart friend and discuss the problem, and use that friend's response in her answer." Precisely. In a normal setting that is called collaboration. Calling on some skilled person, getting their ideas, understanding, and then articulating those ideas under pressure—how can that be considered a bad thing?

What you want from a candidate in return is an *approach*. You do NOT want a solution, per se; rather, you want the candidate to describe the meta-solution: how they would go about solving the problem, *not* the solution itself. The candidate's expression of the approach is far more revealing of her future success in problem solving.

Crafting a Culture

It isn't sufficient to pick excellent leaders and outstanding team members. You must constantly attend to the care and feeding of the culture that permeates that group and the company around it as well.

In most cases you will be starting with an organization culture that has a strong immune response to problem solving. "But we solve problems every day, and have been doing that since the beginning of time, right?" Wrong. Organizations typically work hard on the back end of a problem to make the fire go away. By and large, most organizations rarely solve a problem at its roots, in a sustainable way, which is what this book is all about.

You may have heard the popular anecdote from Stephen Covey's *7 Habits of Highly Effective People.* In one story, he tells the tale of a woodcutter who has been hard at work chopping down trees for hours. His progress is slowing because the saw blade he is using is getting dull. A visitor walks by and suggests that he sharpen his saw to go faster. "I don't have time," says the woodcutter. He is too busy cutting wood to stop.

The pressure and the pace of modern corporate life creates a "speed at all cost" type of culture that works decidedly against a true problem-solving culture. Yet at the same time there is a danger in swinging the pendulum to the opposite extreme where *analysis paralysis* sets in. I do not suggest the solution to the paradox is to force someone who is darned good at cutting wood to stop doing that. Rather, I will suggest that a partner be added alongside the woodcutter to think about and implement a saw sharpening system. That doesn't threaten or annoy the woodcutter in any way. In fact, most woodcutters would deeply appreciate the use of a sharp saw all the time. In an ideal world the woodcutter tells his other woodcutter friends how great his life is now with sharp saws from his good friend and partner, causing them to seek out other saw sharpeners, and so on, in turn generating a virtuous cycle that raises the whole level of productivity in the woodcutter industry, and driving deep interest in other technologies that have a bearing on cutting wood.

Even the term we use for the role "problem solver" can be...well...a problem, especially for others in the organization. The phrase implies (1) these people are much smarter than you are, and (2) they are about to change what you have been doing successfully for years. It is a mental model that will be ingrained in the vast majority of business people teams you will encounter.

The fear of change is present in everyone. The good news for the recipient of change in a problem-solving context is that changes are rarely complete reinventions of what was done before. The vast majority of solutions I have witnessed really involved humans doing more or less the same function they did before, but in the new world they do it informed by data and analysis. The human in charge, stemming from a new ability to see into the function in a richer way, enacts the subtle but profound changes that ensue. As I mentioned in chapter 4, visualization can play an extremely helpful role in showing all of the stakeholders how and why the new solution came about.

Whether you like it or not, the problem-solving team will have an internal brand—so we might as well make it a good one. In my own experience with these teams, the best approach is to make the team's successes and failures very transparent by talking about them, publicly, at every opportunity. Talking about failures does not mean highlighting where you've screwed up, but rather how you have failed gracefully, the lessons learned from that experience, and how you you've retooled as a result.

The best teams form alliances with related corporate functions. Many organizations of size have internal Lean Thinking or Business Excellence teams, and these groups can be very helpful partners in problem identification and solving. Commit to integration by actually drawing on paper how you will interface with these teams and possibly share resources.

Problem Solving and Creativity

At first glance it would seem that problem solving isn't very creative, but rather, it is simply making the best play with the cards that have been dealt. It is a clear-cut process of applying rules again and again until the solution is apparent. That is true, but to suggest that creativity and innovation is not an important part of the problem-solving equation is not true at all. When we build models, we become professional "pretenders"—creating fake replicas of some system—a company or a process—as a way to pretend we are driving the real system in God-like fashion. The pretense, via simulation, gives us insights into the behavior of the real system under a variety of imagined conditions. And so it is through this process that you can engage in some creative thinking through *juxtaposition*.

Juxtaposition: two or more objects placed in close proximity such that the contrast reveals something about each object

Juxtaposition in business is a way to get creative thinking moving along a thought sequence that causes us to question long-held beliefs about how our businesses work. Here are some examples of juxtapositions in business:

- What if the CEO of our biggest competitor ran our company? How would it be run differently?
- If UPS ran our supply chain, what would that look like?
- If Steve Jobs walked into our company tomorrow, what would he do first?
- If an entire management team from another industry were forced to take over the firm, what emphasis would they pursue?

These are not only thought experiments but they are also triggers for a whole sequence of activities that could prove invaluable to the company—calling into question everything you do and why you do it that way. There is no doubt that organizations do lots of things well and should keep doing it—but the mere act of asking the questions reveals potential weaknesses and systemic or structural fissures. One might even pursue the formal process of simulating the company under different leadership styles in the same way that war historians play out long ago battles with different generals at the helm. You will be amazed at how often the creative juices start to flow when people are free to think in crazy ways, spurred by an exercise that forces them to imagine situations that don't exist.

The technical sandbox that we introduced in chapter 5 serves as a constant but subtle reminder to the team that collaboration is paramount. Everyone on the team is identified by the sandbox and is responsible for contributing technical content to it. This is particularly important for smart creative types as many have a natural tendency to work as lone wolves.

Over time, the models created in the sandbox represent cherished assets of the company, and the team are the honored custodians of those assets. Somewhere there should be a list and description of all of the products of the team—a virtual trophy case of problem-solving achievements.

The best teams also adopt a culture of quickness, by recognizing that a "close enough" solution developed in two days is superior to a perfect solution that takes two months. This is not in any way a compromise on quality but rather a choice of completeness of the solution—good judgments about what level of detail to include in the model and what elements to leave out. Problem-solving teams must move at the same speed the business moves in order to be relevant.

A culture of quickness also implies a high degree of productivity, and nothing kills productivity faster than meetings. The knee-jerk reaction of "let's have a meeting" to any arising issue or the dreaded standing-meeting-every-Monday drains productive time from the teams. Not only that, meetings are in direct conflict with the Agile methodology, which tends to promote frequent but brief huddles throughout the day as opposed to the sluggish ceremony of the typical meeting.

Picking Problems

Having a high-performing problem-solving team is like holding a very powerful fire hose. Where do you point it to do the most good? How can I avoid pointing it poorly and doing more damage? It is essential to give some thought to the kinds of problems the team should and shouldn't work on.

It may sound unsophisticated to wander around the company and ask each team to list their top 10 challenges, but this is actually a good place to start. If you took the challenges at face value, it would indeed be a sophomoric exercise. Good problem solvers look past the narrow way the challenge is stated to seek the root of the problem.

Let me give you an example.[3] Bernie from Accounting says, "Our working capital costs are way higher than our peers' in the industry." After some checking, you confirm that this is indeed the case, as supported by reliable data. However, Bernie's observation begs the question: is there something unique about our firm that necessitates a higher than average working capital, say, an inventory policy that ensures on-time delivery better than our competitors? If this is the case, the problem is not a high working capital cost but rather a choice within the perceived trade-off between two noble goals in tension: keeping inventories low and maintaining excellent customer service through on-time delivery. This is a decidedly different (and more useful) frame around the problem than simply solving Bernie's introductory challenge. Were we to adopt high working capital as our sole problem to solve, then solve it, all we would really do is shift the problem from a financial domain to a customer domain (reducing inventories leading to frequent shortages), possibly making the impact on the company as a whole worse. This is the fire hose pointed away from the fire and instead knocking down perfectly good walls and overturning furniture. The antidote for this is the same kind of "end to end" thinking we introduced earlier in this chapter as an attractive attribute in candidates for the problem-solving team. Instinctively these people will go much deeper into a problem beyond the observations of individuals. Here we look to the disciplines of engineering and science, in which depth and clarity in hypothesis formulation is considered a foundational principle. A well-rounded hypothesis would explore the trade-off between too much inventory at a high working capital cost that Bernie mentioned and too little inventory that causes problems such as stockouts. A model that plots a chart of an overall "goodness" metric for the company might exhibit a mountain-top shape when each extreme of inventory—high or low—forms the x-axis. There may also be conditions that would cause the mountain to "tilt" left or right as other factors change over time.

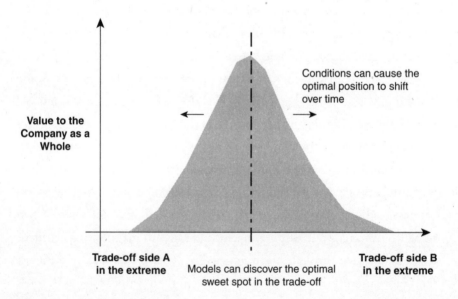

Figure 7.1 Modeling trade-offs

Applying *deep* thinking to a list of stated observations across the company is a very healthy exercise—one that I recommend company leadership does at least once a year, if not more frequently. The list itself is revealing. Are there common problems from one division to another?

Are there surprising skills needed to generate solutions? What potential methodologies rise to the top? What didn't make the list that we thought should have been there? The list is a valuable survey of activity and intellectual property that leadership should recognize and discuss.

At least one of the columns on the list will be related to the value of solving the problem, and another the cost of generating the solution. You might be surprised by my perspective on that, which is don't be overly precise. Good problems generally have a lopsidedly positive return on investment (ROI), qualitatively and quantitatively, and efforts to make this highly accurate so that one can choose problem A over problem B are a waste of valuable resources. Choose problems that make an *obvious material difference* to the organization, financially and strategically.

The governing board of an organization is a constituency that should never be ignored in seeking out challenges to add to the list. Effective boards not only see problems with an end-to-end perspective but also maintain clear goals for the organization—goals that are really just problems in disguise (e.g., "how do we meet ___ performance target?").

Once the list is compiled, I recommend making it highly visible throughout the organization. It should be discussed frequently, and results against those problems posted for all to see. Allow others to comment—some of your best solution ideas could come from unexpected corners of the company.

The Commons

I believe that the consulting firm where I work is somewhat unique in that on any given day, we get to see the inner workings of a dazzling array of industries: semiconductors to consumer goods, high technology to government departments. The experience is fascinating—our front row seat on the thrill ride of everyday global commerce allows us to observe the intriguing similarities of problems across the spectrum. Equally amusing are the perspectives from the individual organizations on how their problems are somewhat unique and more challenging than others'.

I don't mean to diminish the complexity of challenges in certain industries. To be sure, managing a drug pipeline in a pharmaceutical company or optimizing a portfolio of drilling assets for an upstream energy firm are devilishly hard problems. However, firms often take the idea of uniqueness a bit too far, and rarely study firms and problems outside of their industry to make useful connections.

To that end, let us look at a few classes of problems we call *The Commons*, owing to their appearance time and time again as we work with firms across the globe. At some scale there is no doubt that your firm has one or more of these problems, even if it isn't widely recognized. That's okay, because the best problem-solving teams go well beyond the obvious, "in your face" problems of the day to seek out problems that are hidden behind the noise of everyday bustle.

Cultural Resistance to Problem Solving

It may surprise you that there is a great deal of resistance to solving problems. No one will ever come out and say, "I don't want you to solve this problem," but their actions lead to the same result. In many cases, well-intentioned people will kill problem solving by attempting to perfect it to death. Here are a few common roadblocks:

"This is not our most important problem." It is rare to be working on *the* big hairy killer problem at any given moment. Problems are selected for solution based on all kinds of criteria, not just the size and impact. Unfortunately, diverting teams away from carefully selected problems to the "big" problems of the day can stop good efforts that are underway.

"The path to a solution isn't very clear." Often people think that problem solving is a project activity like any other—with well-defined steps and timelines. Agile development simply doesn't work that way, and an attempt to put artificially precise time steps on problem-solving work is a colossal waste of time. Problem solving

isn't immune to good project management, but it isn't like building a house either.

"We've already solved that." Solutions that have not come as a result of the careful kind of process that has been described here might "seem" like a solution, but in fact is not likely sustainable—more like a Band-Aid than surgery. Remember that the solution itself is not necessarily the most important outcome—the exhibits built along the way (hypothesis, qualitative model, quantitative model, data, diagrams, notes, interviews) are just as important to preserve.

"Our data isn't very good. Let's wait until we have better data." You might as well wait forever—perfect (or even very good) data is a luxury that few problems have. Let the process continue until it is crystal clear that a viable solution is impossible with the current state of data. You might be surprised at how far you can go, and in a worst case, you will have evaluated exactly what data would be necessary to make the solution work, which is valuable in itself.

"I don't think the business case for that problem is very strong." Fine. Where's the proof? The person making this charge should be just as compelled to make the case against going after the problem as the one promoting a solution approach. Yet it seems the case in many organizations that the wave of a hand by the right executive is all that is needed to kill a solution, while attacking a problem is subjected to the rigor of a formal business case. It is time for some balance here.

...and here are a few antidotes to consider:

Recruit the naysayers. Some naysayers can make the best problem-solving team members, although careful handling is a must. I once had a gentleman challenge the accuracy of a model we built for a chemical manufacturer. "You'll never get those yield equations right," he grumbled. You guessed it—we immediately set up a meeting with him to formulate the yield equations. He became the model's biggest champion because that part of the model *was his signature.*

Challenge the default position. "As opposed to what?" are my favorite four words. "That model won't work/isn't helpful/shouldn't proceed" is in effect arguing for whatever the status quo solution happens to be. I'll never forget a lively meeting with a group of executives in the construction industry. We were debating the creation of a demand forecasting model with a wide variety of views on how to proceed. The CEO finally blew the whistle and said, "Hey, folks, keep in mind how we forecast now. We do that manually, and it's little better than an educated guess. Even if this model is only mediocre, it is a far better approach than we use now. And I think if it does have faults, we can fix those over time." The room went silent for a while, then we proceeded to piece the model's concept together.

Ignore and proceed anyway. It wouldn't be the first time that a bold team ignored the conventional wisdom and set out to prove the detractors wrong. History suggests that skunkworks projects, running under the radar, are some of the most valuable work companies do.

I am not suggesting that challenges to problem solving aren't legitimate—most are. However thoughtful, constructive modifications to problem solving are preferred over quick from-the-hip judgments that slow progress. Every argument, pro or con, must live on its merits through logic and data, no matter what title you have.

Tradeoffs

As mentioned in Bernie's example earlier, the absence of data creates fertile ground for poorly formed mental models to take hold in groups of people. Nowhere is this more evident than in trade-offs that become the stuff of company lore. "We can't enter that market, however promising," a company executive once told me. "Because the credit capacity of customers there is weak. Some accounts will pay us very late or not at all. It isn't worth the effort."

A fair point, and I certainly cannot argue with his logic or data, although some people in that same organization took issue with his stance. That said, he wasn't stating the problem quite right. What he is really saying is that there is a *trade-off* between expanding their markets into promising areas and sticking with known markets where the financial parameters are more favorable. Trade-offs are a class of problems quite amenable to a scientific viewpoint. After we took a deeper dive into the hypothesis of new market entry, we did indeed find an optimal means for entering new and uncertain markets—not zero entry, and not entry with wild abandon, but a carefully validated approach that maintains the upside and avoids the downside.

When you hear of someone advocating one end of a trade-off or another with no data, that alone is a clue that you likely have a solvable, valuable problem on your hands.

The Greying Workforce Problem

There is an odd demographic at work in a surprisingly vast array of industries. Knowledgeable, experienced leaders in a technical discipline are in their 50s, a decade or so away from retirement. Eager, motivated talent in its 20s and 30s are coming in. The generation gap in-between is minimal, setting up a talent shortage problem in the coming decade that could kill the organization—a train wreck in slow motion. The problem has become so ominous in the energy industry that it has generated its own nickname—"The Great Crew Change."

The current generation of technical leaders rarely write their knowledge down in some meaningful way that others can use. Why should they? "Just ask Sue down the hall. She knows everything about ___." In spite of a great deal of work under the banner of something called Knowledge Management, we have failed to do any more than create a few random encyclopedias that no one ever reads.

The solution here, in a word, is *simulation*. Creating a simulation model of a particular aspect of the company's operations is a forcing function that causes technical leaders to act as SMEs for the simulation's creation. All of the artifacts of the model-building process serve as the blueprint of the model, but also are a clear, graphical depiction of the knowledge in the SME's head. In attacking the greying workforce problem, it almost doesn't matter what the underlying problem is.

Now place that against the manner in which the new generation of talent learns something new. In my younger days this meant reading an endless list of manuals and following around a veteran for a few months. Not anymore. Today's generation learns by doing; they have no fear of mistakes and are quite comfortable with the technology. Simulation is a near perfect bridge between the generations, preserving the invaluable institutional knowledge of the firm while feeding it efficiently to the next generation of technical leaders.

Mergers and Acquisitions

One thing that organizations do frequently is buy other organizations, or merge in some form. Successful joins are surprisingly rare, even in our modern, sophisticated world of corporate thinking. A range of studies put the failure rate of mergers and acquisitions (M&A) between 70 percent and 90 percent.[4] The statistics form the tip of an iceberg whose mass is below the waterline: the tension between the need to grow beyond an organic rate against the difficulties and complexities of stitching two or more organizations together.

M&A is a stark example of how spreadsheets are insufficient tools to deal with the complexity of the problem at hand. Break apart any merger or acquisition today, and what do you see?—a beehive of well-intentioned people generating a mass of disparate stand-alone spreadsheets. Sheer luck is the only way that approach works.

I have seen (and have been a part of) a few large M&A events where the principals took the wise, bold step of *modeling* the integration. I don't mean just a computer model, but deliberately, systematically, and objectively describing the *calculus* of the combination on paper. Not only did this exquisitely shape the work of the merger integration teams but it also allowed leadership to tell a consistent and comprehensive story to analysts and investors outside of the company.

Operational Risk

Risk is the water of the corporate world. You cannot live without it, but too much can kill you. Every organization on the planet deals with risk. The question is, do you deal with risk in an intuitive way, or in a data-driven way? Intuition will only get you so far, as risks deal with layered probabilities, and probabilities without data are just guesses.

Operational risk is a special category that deals with the performance of some system in real-world conditions. Leadership will often ask, "how likely is it that __ (bad thing) will happen?" That is the wrong question, as it would lead us to guess the probability of this scenario or that—the flawed prediction style that we highlighted in chapter 1. The better alternative is to represent every possible state in the system (every possible combination of input parameters),[5] then assess—through a comprehensive model of the system—how many of these possible states lead to a bad, or perhaps a very bad outcome.

Every possible state in the system? Why, that would be infinity!

It might seem that way, but is rarely the case. Usually, good SMEs can narrow the cases down to a few million *plausible* combinations. Once that is accomplished, the very bad outcomes represent a small number of special cases among the many where the metrics went way South. The proper response to the leadership's question above then becomes, "I can't predict how likely, but in 22 of 100,000 cases this really bad thing happened." Deep examination of the 22 special cases, including their implications, will inspire the right kind of countermeasure discussion around the company.

Competition

If you take a look at professional sports teams and the average corporation, you will see many similarities. Both are keenly aware of their markets.

Both invest in technology to improve their products and streamline delivery. Both lord over their talent, managing it like the key asset that it is. But there is one thing that separates professional sports from most companies: sports teams study their competition.

Now, when I say study the competition, I *really* mean study. They watch endless game films, develop statistical profiles of the key player opponents, model team performance under a variety of factors—was it a home or away game? At night? Out west? What was the attendance like at game time? The temperature on the field?

Most companies do the bare minimum—they take an occasional look at the competing product line, gather information on pricing, perhaps even hire a few folks from the competitor to get some inside knowledge. Many, particularly in industrial B2B markets, shockingly assert, "We really don't have any competition."

On the other hand, a few very progressive-minded organizations have taken problem solving to a new and interesting level by modeling the *problem* of competition. Almost everyone has competition of one sort or another, even governments and nonprofits. How does the competitor respond to key events? What is their capacity? Internal costs? How do they think about pricing? Strategic decisions?

You might be thinking, "We have no idea about any of that." That is unlikely to be the case. In many of the organizations I speak with, there is at least an employee or two who formerly worked for competitor X. People from competing organizations interact at trade shows. Companies make speeches and give public presentations that reveal how they think. Industry groups collect anonymized data, at times under the banner of benchmark development, on the industry as a whole, but it is not impossible to ferret out how individual companies might be positioned through the aggregated data set. Again, our standard here is not a high level of precision, but close enough so that insights into the minds of our competitors is a degree or two better than guesswork (or worse, ignoring the competition completely).

A healthy exercise is to *role play* a competitor. Sports teams do this as well by lining up offenses against defenses that "look like" the way the opposing team plays (and vice versa). Try it yourself...grab a handful of your smartest executives or board members and have them in secret devise an attack plan against the firm. Once the plan is developed, have them reveal it and juxtapose that directly against your stated strategy. This will clearly reveal weak points in your defenses and might also point out a hole that your offense can exploit.

Another suggestion—create a competitor...*in silicon*. Computer simulations are often the most effective way of crafting organizations and their behaviors. The process of creating a competitor—perhaps devised "Frankenstein-like" from pieces and parts of real companies you know well—is often just as valuable as the simulation model itself. Once developed, you could stress test that synthetic competitor under a variety of market conditions. Moreover, when a brand new entrant comes into the market, you'll be ready to systematically assess their effect.

Good firms react to competitors' moves. Great firms make a routine practice of studying the competition analytically through models.

Manual and Rote to Automatic and Intelligent

What do your people do? I'm not talking about job descriptions or titles; rather, I am really talking about what they actually do all day long, day in and day out. It is a serious question, because too often the answer is that people perform a surprising number of tasks that are very low on the intelligence scale. The shame of it is that this robs those same people of the time to perform true value-added tasks that are best suited for the flexible human brain.

I worked with a company in the marine logistics business on voyage scheduling. Shipments of supplies and equipment would arrive at the shorebase, and an army of dedicated people would ensure that all of the materials were on the right vessel at the right time. The company hardly ever missed a due date, and had a reputation for getting the job done right every time. However, disruptions from weather, land shipment delays, and shipping errors from suppliers were a persistent feature of their daily lives. Again, the sweat of an *extended* army of people would cover exceptional circumstances. Rinse. Repeat the next day.

The whole system revolved around lots of humans performing a number of simple but fairly repeatable tasks. With the right models in place, these tasks could be consigned to algorithms, leaving the humans free to engage in the more human-like work of *interpreting* the voyage schedule and putting some thought into its construction, perhaps thinking ahead to next week's schedule, or the impact of that new customer, or various configurations of the schedule that would optimize the company's fleet. Over time, we constructed a system of models underneath a software system that moved people away from mechanically consistent, rule-based tasks into thinking-centric roles. The company continued to hone its leadership position in the industry, a virtually untouchable first place status today.

The R&D of Problem Solving

Solving problems is serious, highly technical work. It exists in an atmosphere of constant change—in the methods, tools, and applications of the craft across industries. Problem solving done well includes a deliberate effort in R&D to ensure that the practice stays up to date with the science.

Cross-Collaboration

It is easy for a particular industry to fall into the trap of assuming that problem-solving innovations occur within its own industry. That is only a fraction of the innovation sphere; innovations can be found everywhere—you only have to work a little harder to distill an innovation in a different industry down into its fundamental function to see how this could be applied in an alternative setting. I call the process of actively seeking new ways to solve problems by trolling other industries *cross-collaboration*, introduced briefly in the previous chapter.

This came home to me once on a visit to a pharmaceutical company that was addressing the problem of risk-weighted investment in compounds in its drug portfolio. The company had developed a sophisticated way of assessing the value of investing one dollar to advance drug A versus using that same dollar to advance drug B, all in an environment of tremendous uncertainty.

The next morning I flew back home to Houston to visit with an upstream oil and gas company. They were trying to understand how the company executes sequencing decisions—whether to continue drilling on this well, versus putting the same resources on another well 50 miles away. Once the parochial attributes were stripped away, the pharmaceutical firm and the oil and gas firm were dealing with the same problem! This was no random accident—similarities exist across countless organizations and much can be learned from understanding diverse applications.

Finding New Methods

Ever heard of data envelopment analysis? How about principal component analysis? Agent-based modeling? If you are like most people, you are not in continuous contact with the research or academic communities that are working on new ways to solve problems. New methods arise every day, and old methods are being updated.

A particular field to watch for is a specialized branch of Operations Research called Management Science. This is concerned with the practical application of methods to real-world problems, especially areas of operations and strategy. The Management Science journal *Informs* is quite readable for those outside of academia.

Check out the companion website to the book, found at http://www. business-laboratory.com/profitfromscience. I will use the website as a forum to routinely review promising new methodologies and describe how they work.

Infusing Analytical Thinking Everywhere

High-performance problem-solving teams are one part of the makeup of a problem-solving company culture. The other is the spread of scientific thinking across the organization, getting everyone to think in data-driven ways. Systematic, objective, and methodical treatment of things we observe in everyday business activity is by no means the exclusive territory of the problem-solving team.

Company-wide campaigns encouraging scientific thinking not only help generate ideas for problems to solve but also create fertile ground for problem-solving teams to get work done. Problem-solving cultures are more engaging places to work, and have the reinforcing effect of attracting more and more smart creatives to the company.

Selling *Problem Solving*

If you are fortunate enough to have created a strong problem-solving culture, you have something to brag about. Why not tell your customers and suppliers about it? It doesn't mean you have to reveal company secrets, nor does it mean that you are somehow admitting that you aren't perfect. What it does mean is that you are building a smart, resilient, lasting capability to make the organization better, problem by problem. Customers and suppliers respect transparency and sophistication.

Chapter Summary

Great problem-solving teams are not simply built. They are *engineered* for high performance. That starts with the special and often misunderstood set of skills needed by the team leaders and members. It continues with the proper selection of problems for the team to engage, and creating a culture that is amenable to analytics.

If you follow the guidelines and recommendations in this chapter, you will be well on your way to forming an institutional capability for problem solving that remains with the organization for decades to come—the kind of capability that even customers and suppliers can come to appreciate as a benefit to doing business with you.

So what next?

CHAPTER 8

Implications for the Future

A ncient science has given us a perspective on business problems that feels astonishingly new. The world around us has endless features, now easily recognizable. What started with a review of the historical role of science in our business lives, then wound circuitously through a treatise on data, methods, and visualization. Along the way we talked technology, became empowered, and built teams.

It is an ideal time to reflect on what this means to us, how our future will be different with this potent way of thinking. What is in store for our lives now?

Problem solvers are uniquely positioned to play a prominent role in the future advancement of our organizations. With luck, a dose of speculative thinking will prepare us for the unknown.

Let me first suggest that we may be nearing an inflection point with regard to the confluence of science and technology to solve problems analytically. If we look at the history of past technological developments where the progression of capability lurched forward, each case was marked by the emergence of a collection of imperfect first-generation systems followed by second- and third-generation more reliable and useful systems performing the same function. The reinforcing loop of fail, learn, fail a little bit less, learn some more, is a distinct feature of the buildup to an explosion in the field.

With this as our framework, I believe that we see evidence today that we are in the nascent stages of just such an eruption. Here are just a few data points to consider:

1. **Siri**. The combination of voice recognition technology with methods for meaningful interpretation of verbal commands has created a whole new category of intelligence. Siri wasn't perfect at its first introduction on the iPhone, and still isn't perfect today, but the

integration of these two technologies set in motion a wave of development of true intelligence in software.

2. **Wolfram Alpha**. The result of more than a decade of work by scientist Stephen Wolfram, WolframAlpha.com is one of the premier applications of natural language processing, ushering in an era of computable knowledge.

3. **Nest**. Who would have thought that a thermostat would represent the perfect confluence of machine learning, product design, user interfaces, and sensor technology? Nest sets the standard for so-called "smart" consumer devices.

4. **Watson**. The IBM technology uses something that you will hear a lot about in future years: cognitive processing. While most smart applications are programmed in code, cognitive processing seeks to learn from a combination of programmed and observed behavior, getting software to work less like a machine and more like the human brain. It should be noted that in Watson's first tests with the popular *Jeopardy!* game, performance (against a human competitor) was terrible. A few years later, in 2011, Watson beat the best two human players of *Jeopardy!* in a three-way match.

The underlying principle of many of these developments of the future is a redefinition of our notions of what is "smart" and "intelligent." When we see a traffic light that uses road-based sensors to time its cycles, we think of that as a smart traffic light, right? That is because such a traffic light has evolved a degree of intelligence over the previous generation of dumb traffic lights that stepped through their cycles using only a mechanical timer (which in turn was an evolution over human-operated traffic lights when they were first invented in the 1860s).

More broadly, we currently think of smart systems and devices in two ways: (1) those things which take into account a range of electronically sensed conditions and perform their task accordingly, or (2) a system that replaces or extends a mechanical function with software-based functions.

A toaster with a CPU inside is a *smart* toaster. A fast food restaurant that uses technology to process and display customer orders is a *smart* restaurant. A portable phone that runs software is a *smart* phone. A building that adjusts the temperature and lighting floor by floor based upon time of day, season, and occupancy is a *smart* building.

I believe that we are already beginning to consider these kinds of systems to be normal, everyday systems. What we consider "smart" in the future will be redefined to the next logical evolution of intelligence, as evidenced by three features: (1) learning, (2) prediction, and (3) human-to-machine role exchange.

Systems That Learn

Most smart systems we use are created by developers from a base of computer code. The code can adapt, in an if-then-else sort of way, to data fed to it. Advancement of these systems occurs by adding more if-then-else sorts of rules to account for more kinds of conditions. We already see that we are breaking away from hard-coded systems in favor of systems that adapt as they learn their surroundings and users. Such systems maintain an extensive data history and put that data through learning functions (as discussed in chapter 5) to alter its output. Certain cars are now building learning into their traction control systems to adjust per the driver's road habits.

Prediction, or Systems That Anticipate

Smart systems of the present generation react to inputs around them. One of the definitions of smart in the future will be a system's ability to go beyond mere reaction to forecast future events and align to anticipate and counter the events. The transportation service Uber, for example, uses an algorithm to stage drivers in locations that are the most likely for immediate demand, with so-called supply positioning heat maps. This is one reason Uber can get drivers to customers so quickly "on demand."

Human to Machine

In modern history there has always existed an invisible line demarcating human tasks from machine tasks. Without question, that line continues to move toward the machine, with more and more tasks falling away from humans and into the machine-capable domain. For example, today when you apply for a bank loan, it is highly likely that a series of machines will largely decide whether you qualify or not.

If you buy my argument that we are now at an inflection point of power and capability in analytics used to drive machine-based systems, then it isn't much of a stretch to conclude that tasks we would have *never* considered to be automatable will be precisely that. Look at current developments by Google in self-driving cars,[1] or models used by criminal justice jurisdictions to determine sentencing guidelines for convicted offenders.

The important point for problem solvers is to avoid the self-imposed limitation of "that could never be automated." Such limitations are falling away with increasing regularity these days.

The bottom line is this: the new classification of intelligence has profound implications for problem solvers. Tools and methods for learning and prediction are very likely to improve in power and ease of use. Moreover, tasks once considered the exclusive domain of humans will come into view as candidates for automation.

One useful way to address the future for problem solvers is to break the many development streams into manageable lanes of development so that the whole picture is easier to digest.

Computing

Small, Highly Intelligent Devices

By far the most sweeping changes for problem solvers in the coming years will be in technology, more specifically, those advancements that allow us access to ubiquitous, pervasive computing at very low cost. We see a hint of the future today in a remarkable, very small, inexpensive computer called the Raspberry Pi. Originally created as a tool for educators, hobbyists took the Raspberry Pi on as a quest for injecting computing into everyday life. Applications from weather stations mounted to a balloon, to home control and security, to stage effects, to home-brewed supercomputers flowed from a vibrant community of experimenters, all with a Wi-Fi enabled computer that costs about $30.[2]

These devices may actually be at the forefront of problem solving, collecting data, computing it, and making recommendations to humans or potentially enacting some decisions on its own—such as a self-driving car or a robotically controlled greenhouse. As embedded small-device computing becomes reality, problem solvers must switch roles by imparting problem-solving code into the devices themselves, as opposed to decision models for human consumption. The good news is that the skills to do so are easily transferrable from one to the other.

Virtual Reality

The subject of many a science fiction novel or movie, virtual reality (VR) was hamstrung by irrational hype a decade ago. VR more commonly involves wearing a stereoscopic headset that responds to movement by changing the angle of the view. Turn your head to the right and you get to "see" what is to the right of your position in the virtual world.

Back then, VR headsets were thousands of dollars (if you could even find one for sale on an individual basis). Today, the Oculus Rift, a gold standard for VR headsets, sells for $350. The price of good VR technology has fallen below the inflection point for mass adoption, and the evidence is clear—applications are now emerging in medicine, personal entertainment, remote device control, education, psychotherapy, and architecture.

Google Glass allows computer-generated displays alongside a real scene via a tiny display fitted to an ordinary pair of glasses. This is known as *augmented* reality, where a real world scene is supplmemeted by data about the objects and landscapes increases your understanding of what is happing in your view in real time. Augmented reality is similar in principle to VR, but instead of being immersed in a virtual world, you are working in the real world and guided by information that comes alongside your physical view.

I believe that both virtual and augmented reality will play a role in many of the use cases of simulation that we discussed in previous chapters, notably in MFS exercises.

Cloud Computing

The fixed-to-variable cost advantage of moving compute loads to external server farms gave rise to cloud computing, but the consequence of an inexpensive, flexible means of computing is of particular benefit to problem solvers. By its very nature, problem solving is episodic and transient, which maps perfectly to a cloud solution. Cloud-based infrastructure for both computing and data can be stood up, expanded, contracted, and shut down completely on a moment's notice.

Concerns over security are holding many organizations back from a more extensive embrace of cloud computing. Security and data loss concerns are legitimate, but slightly overblown. Many cloud critics are not sufficiently recognizing that the same kinds of vulnerabilities exist behind the firewall as well.

There is great interest in the industry and a strong financial motivation for solving the cloud security and reliability problem; therefore, I believe that the problem will be solved in time. Once that is happens, cloud computing will be the norm for problem-solving teams, where physical server-based computing behind the firewall will be the exception.

Super Computing for the Masses

Supercomputing used to be the exclusive domain of university research labs or very large corporations. That is no longer true given the advent of grid computing. While grid computing has been with us for quite some time, most software these days is not designed to take advantage of it. True grid computing is creating a single environment where computers work cooperatively on a single problem. You order a book from your favorite online seller—the system breaks different pieces of the transaction up (debiting your credit card, updating your purchase history, placing an order at the distribution center) and processes them on different devices (nodes) instead of handling each instruction sequentially.

In that example, the differences in processing time with grid versus conventional programming are slight. But what if you had to repeat some task like that ten million times? Most simulations are structured in a way that requires lots of small calculations to be performed over and over many times, making grid computing an essential element in tackling very large-scale problems.

The technology for linking many low-cost computers together is now well grounded. The software is beginning to catch up, allowing users to run programs that *automatically* splice their subfunctions across a grid without the need to know the details of how that occurs. Computers will continue to get faster, but in the future we will be able to solve problems with trillions of possible outcomes by leveraging grid computing.

Self-Extending Networks

The extent of special purpose communication networks is often limited by the cost of the infrastructure, coupled with the overhead of regulatory licensing. However, we are just beginning to see self-extending networks—networks comprised of nodes that share bandwidth. Communication then hops along all of the shared infrastructure seamlessly, all while maintaining the security of the individual user.

So, for example, if I place some kind of network node in my car, and another one in my home, I can communicate to devices that can be attached to those nodes. However, if my neighbor has a compatible node, and my neighbor's neighbor, and so on, we can all jointly leapfrog on that common collection of infrastructure.

3D Printing

Another form of "simulation" to emerge in recent years is the advent of 3D printing. By taking an object described in the computer and using an inexpensive machine to generate the equivalent object in the real world, we are in essence solving problems by printing solutions. This in turn gives rise to objects that are in and of themselves a solution, generated by computer code as opposed to the manual construction of each and every physical dimension. The architecture community is already headed in this direction, designing buildings whose forms follow a set of equations.

Algorithms as Business Currency

Today, our common notion of value is in accounting assets—cash, machinery, art, license agreements. Sure, there is value in intellectual and intangible property, and we have figured out ways to value that kind of thing. What I suggest is that a new category of assets will become more and more important in the future: algorithms.

As organizations begin to use models for important decisions, the algorithms that underlie those models rise in prominence accordingly, particularly when the models are closely linked to competitive advantage. Here are some algorithms of incalculable value from organizations that we have had the opportunity to work with:

- chemical process reactions in refineries that lead to above-industry-average yields from feedstock
- a rating and ranking system for the field sales force
- calculation of a trigger point for retiring one long-standing product in lieu of its replacement
- real-time pricing formula for a range of industrial products
- rules for retail store location relative to competitive stores in an area
- a specially devised risk-weighting metric applied to compounds progressing through a drug pipeline

An algorithm so important deserves to be identified, archived, documented, and managed in line with its value. Precious few organizations do this.

Data

In a world where measurement is free, data will be boundless. The cost of measurement is already approaching zero, and the trend is very likely to continue. So instead of suppliers and buyers relying on a blind assumption that the load of steel supports headed to the construction project is "in transit," it will be fitted with a device that constantly broadcasts its location (and perhaps its total weight, age, the driver's name, moving speed, and temperature) on the Internet.

Privacy Concerns

The friction in the atmosphere of ubiquitous data at the moment is privacy. Personal records must have some level of control and protection, as well as corporate information that represents a competitive advantage.

Data security technology evolves in cycles over time to meet the threat. Think of your own neighborhood. Some people have elaborate systems for home security, while others do not. There are break-ins on occasion, and these are thwarted for the most part on the more secure houses and are successful on the weaker ones. Now imagine that tomorrow a very robust security system was available to everyone for free. For a while, there are no successful break-ins until a clever burglar figures out how to bypass the system, attacking those homeowners who weren't as good as the rest at installing their free system. Pretty soon the security industry comes up with another, better free security solution, and so on.

Attempts to steal data will never go away, but the hurdle for success for potential thieves will get higher. From what I have observed so far, I believe that the technology industry will be able to maintain a slight edge over the threat to the extent that data collection and sharing will continue to develop unhindered.

Data as Code/Code as Data

Privacy aside, our notions of what data is will continue to advance. Our current mental model of data is that of numbers and strings, such as a table of customer names, addresses, and other profile information. Increasingly, we will start to work with more complex data such as images, which will be just as searchable as traditional data. These graphic objects will be handled as easily as we do strings and numbers today. Search phrases such as "find me an image of a tiger at nighttime where the animal is in a crouched position" will be executed *based on the features of the image itself,* not on the fact that some manual process archives the searchable metadata and tags alongside every image (#tiger #nighttime #crouching).

Perhaps one of the most intriguing concepts in thinking about new forms of data is the code as data/data as code idea—the notion that a piece of executable code, either a short fragment or an entire application can serve as data for a separate system to use for analysis. Let us delve into each of the two aspects, code as data, then data as code, in succession.

In the first case, code as data, a batch of code is treated as a thing stored somewhere and imported into a model for analysis. Once inside a model, the code can be visualized, say, all the connections between subfunctions and they make calls to each other, or perhaps the symbolic data it uses, as it is sequentially transforms it from beginning to end. You could assess whether the code has malicious intent, or perhaps apply lean principles in ways to make it run faster.

The second case, data as code, treats a list of functionally similar code fragments as things to be stored away and used as needed by an active program. Think of "personality modules" that can be added or adapted outside of the program, much like the software equivalent of performance-enhancing chips that one can buy for cars to replace the factory-installed engine control unit, or ECU.

The application of data as code came up in our own work in optimizing a chemical plant. The yield equations for certain chemical reactions vary dramatically as temperature and pressure changes. There was also a seasonal impact, product selection, and which units were active—in short, thousands of variations of the yield equation that did not fit nicely into an algorithm. Moreover, yields change slightly as equipment ages, requiring a tuning process outside of the model. All of these conditions added up to a data as code solution in which the yield code per each variation was kept in a database that the model loaded and executed each time it needed to compute yield.

The Internet

Many people think of the Internet as a thing that was invented once, and now is a stable, permanent fixture of our business and personal lives. But in fact, the Internet is evolving in ways that are useful to problem solvers.

On the Internet, every device (computer, router, switch) attached to it gets a unique address called an Internet Protocol address, or IP address. Starting in the early 1980s, these addresses consisted of four blocks of eight bit decimals, that is, the number 0 to 255. This allows 2^{32} addresses, or approximately 4.3 billion unique addresses for devices. In the late 1990s, the IP structure, called IPv6, was officially expanded to handle 2^{128} addresses, or 340,282,366,920,938,463,463,374,607,431,768,211,456 unique devices (340 undecillion). IPv6 is only recently coming into widespread use, but its implications are that countless consumer and industrial devices can feasibly be brought onto the Internet: cars, industrial pumps, appliances, clothing, bridges.

The fact that a device now has an IP address where it did not before, is not interesting by itself. However, most devices get an IP address because it knows lots of information about itself, and can then communicate that local knowledge to another computing device that has a model within it. A model that is connected, say, to every refrigerator in a particular region could perform calculations about the state of refrigeration (energy use, contents of the unit, rate of entry/exit) that simply could not be feasible without such communication.

Beyond devices, organizations as a whole are being encouraged to get into the act. In 2012, noted scientist and software CEO Stephen Wolfram proposed a ".data" top-level domain (TLD) alongside the more familiar .com, .org, .net, and so on.[3] The .data TLD would house computable data about the associated domain. So www.ford.data, for example, would have a corpus of easily readable data structures about every vehicle in its product lineup, every dealer in the world, recall information and investor figures. www.redcross.data would be the "go to" place for information on global disasters in real time, with structured information (nicely formatted tables easily readable by a computer) on how the Red Cross is involved in each one. If every organization began to adopt the .data TLD, this would take one of the most problematic and time-consuming barriers to problem solving—data collection—out of the way in many cases.

Knowledge Systems

One of the fastest growing categories of software these days is the knowledge application. I use the word knowledge here as at present there is no catchy name for this collection of highly intelligent functions backed by a massive repository of information. The basic framework of these applications is the same—they take a natural language question in, via voice or typed command, structure the words into a logical form that code can digest, then use a hidden but substantial data corpus in the back end to match the knowledge they have to the request.

It is important to note that these systems are distinctly different from using keywords in a search phrase to look at sites on the Web that match those keywords with some statistical frequency. Knowledge systems know the meaning of your question. So where the question "What is my mother's brother's sister's cousin?" would confuse a search engine, a knowledge system would supply the *one* precisely correct answer (first cousin once removed) given its corpus of genealogical relationships.

Knowledge systems solve problems (stated as a single question) in an automated way, giving us a first glimpse at machine-based intelligence.

As of this writing there are several products in this space: Wolfram Alpha, Apple's Siri, Viv from Viv Labs, IBM's Watson, and Google Now. Most of these are aimed at mildly amusing consumer applications for voice control and queries, but the implication for problem solvers is much more profound.

Knowledge systems hold the promise that any given member of an organization, with the right level of information credentials, could ask clear, natural language questions and get sensible answers in return. The corpus of knowledge is the organization's own data and models, systematized under a knowledge system. This will in turn give rise to a culture where everyone is asking instant questions all the time, and using the answers to drive further understanding of company operations.

New Problems

One great benefit of being a problem solver is that there is a seemingly endless stream of problems (challenges, opportunities) coming our way, each wave bringing more complexity and exotic wrinkles than we could have anticipated. We cannot predict the future with any degree of certainty, but it is a healthy exercise to speculate on classes of future problems based upon the limited evidence we see today.

Cyber Defense

Having seen the inside of a large financial services organization deal with the problem of cyber defense, I am convinced that this is fertile ground for much better solutions than we have today. In essence, cyber defense at the moment involves building very high thick walls around the information city. However, for commerce to exist, you must build gates to let people in and out. Each gate has a guard, checking the entrants the best they can. The bad guys get in directly through the gates, through cracks in the walls or by co-opting a good person's credentials, hoping the guard doesn't catch them. Stronger cyber defense year upon year translates into building higher, thicker walls and putting more guards at each gate. Meanwhile, ten times more new bad guys come of age, much more clever than the corrupt parents who raised them.

The current methods of cyber defense evolution are insufficient to meet the threat. Cyber defense is prime territory for a complete redesign in the spirit of what Nassim Nicholas Taleb, author of *The Black Swan*, calls antifragile. Taleb defines antifragile systems as those mechanisms that *get stronger* under volatility, chaos, or exceptional circumstance, not simply ward off its effects. This in turn implies a much more proactive role for cyber defense, perhaps better termed cyber offense, which might gather information—learning about an attacker to use against him at a later date, which is akin to jumping over the wall to harm the enemy with superior weaponry. To do so will require sophistication borne of the methods we introduced in chapter 2, which invites capable problem solvers into the presently exclusive, product-oriented domain of cyber defense.

Surge

Does it strike you as odd that here in this modern, erudite age we still routinely run out of stuff? We see this constantly in our daily lives—the restaurant that runs out of a favorite dish, the store that cannot seem to stock that special toy for Christmas, the coffee shop that, of all things, runs out of lids for the cups!

Our mental models suggest that large, sophisticated organizations have mastered their supply chains thoroughly. Highly computerized operations deliver the goods at the right time in the right amounts, taking into account the seasonal buying patterns of the consumer. Yet, stockouts are common, frustrating the customer and denying the organization needed revenue (just at the time it could likely charge a premium!). Why?

The answer is that we do not grasp the repercussions of *surge*: natural up-cycles in business. Our choice to optimize our processes at some nominal level of production secretly dooms us to fail when those same processes are stretched by a surge in workflow. We can easily point to numerous examples of surge-crashing systems: natural disaster response, Christmas season supply chains, airline delays that ripple across a continent. When confronted, many leaders of these systems respond with a shrug and an anemic "That's just the way things are," as if weak performance under surge conditions were an inevitable state.

I believe that we can master the unique calculus of surge when and where it arises with a correct dose of simulation and analysis, using stress tests to reveal weaknesses and provide solutions to correct those weaknesses.

Forecasting

Forecasting has been with us since the dawn of time, when the learned men and women of the ages started conjecturing about future events as driven by some kind of reliable pattern. So how is this a *new* problem? It isn't a new problem, really, but rather we see a new way of looking at this age-old problem through newfound granularity.

Most national surveys or polls conducted in the United States use a sample size of about 1,000, and these surveys are said to accurate within +/– 3 percent. Think about that for a minute—a country of 322 million people, whose opinion is deduced accurately from 1,000 randomly drawn people? That is 0.00031 percent!

Accurate forecasts from tiny samples seem astonishing, but they have to do with the theory of statistical sampling...the accuracy is shown to increase only marginally as the sample size increases from 1,000, so poll designers continue to use this figure. This extends into the nonexpert world of organizations—when developing a forecast over a large population of customers or markets, we tend to aggregate by some convenient grouping, such as zip code (postcode), county, or district. Aggregation gets us so far (e.g., the 3% band above), but what if you could sample *every possible entity* in question? We call this *exhaustive* forecasting.

The availability of highly granular data is reaching the point at which exhaustive forecasting is feasible. In my own work, I was once asked to generate a forecast of votes in an election across a population of 500,000 eligible voters. Our results were far more accurate than had been seen before. We were separately asked to develop a forecast of UK energy consumption across that country's 28.5 million homes and buildings. The energy forecast represented a step change in the level of accuracy, derived from data compiled on each and every individual building.

Offloading Humans

If you happen to run a large organization, or a team within an organization of more than a handful of people, try the following experiment: document what they do every day—not each and every motion, but rather the functions they perform. I believe what you will find (because it is so universal) is that most of the functions, even those performed by higher level positions, are rote, mechanical tasks that involve almost no thinking and are certainly devoid of any creativity. Then ask the question "Why don't you spend more time thinking about your work?" The common response is "Because I don't have time with all the other work I do."

We have not even begun to tap the productivity that is available to us, because we have dumbed down the work to an infinite number of puerile tasks:

1. The sales manager who has to "go over" the sales figures every month instead of attending to areas that are doing poorly by migrating practices from the areas doing well.
2. The operations manager who is just recovering from solving an inventory crisis, instead of thinking about the production system as a whole, and mapping its elements.
3. The financial director who manually makes endless PowerPoint slides in advance of the annual meeting instead of researching new valuation techniques.

If we take an honest look at most of the work humans do inside organizations, a very large chunk of that could be automated with the right kinds of bespoke analysis tools. We call this *offloading*, because its intent is *never* to replace humans, but rather to rechannel humans into what humans do far better than computers can do: creatively think about the systems and behaviors around them and how those things could all work in a better way.

Collaboration

It is imperative that all parts of an organization collaborate. This is so easy to say, yet so difficult to do. Analytical models can facilitate more efficient, focused collaboration. Here's how: by running models over and over, observing their responses, and debating the implications of model results under a set of initial conditions. We will talk a lot about the logic and data behind the model, and how closely that represents the real system. Hypotheses, control groups, and validation will be words that will enter the lexicon of corporate strategy and decision-making. In short, the "show me the model" will be the new norm that follows an idea.

Novel Metrics

We are accustomed to financial and operational metrics that are used to drive businesses—inventories, revenues, order-to-cash cycle time. In the future, expect to see new metrics emerge in our models that reflect the balance that organizations are seeking with the expectations of a new world of consumers and investors. I believe that we will find ways to quantify heretofore softer measures such as sustainability and environmental responsibility, and that this capability will in turn allow us to play investment dollars off against improvements along these dimensions.

Transformation of Traditional Business Models through Analytics

Analytics has a peculiar ability to completely upend traditional businesses. Any given company that is built upon traditional assets is a candidate for disruptive change through a properly applied dose of analytics.

Dr. Richard Santulli, a mathematician, pioneered the concept of the fractional jet service using math models of supply and demand to describe how it could work.[4] The fractional jet business is now a thriving, multibillion-dollar industry, made possible, in large part, by a mathematical model.

Amazon, NetFlix, and Uber all rely heavily on analytics to distance themselves from their traditional counterparts. This trend is likely to continue long into the future.

Redefinition of the Role of CEO

I love chess. It always amazes me how such simple rules for piece movements can give rise to matches of such extraordinary complexity and drama. Often I see corporate strategy analogized as a chess game. On the surface, that seems right—managers adeptly try to outthink their opponents in a rich interplay of competing strategies and asset positions.

However, critical analysis casts grave doubt on this analogy. CEOs (or anyone in senior leadership) rarely have the ability to command a direct reaction to a competitive attack in the market, or even to oversee core business transactions. Economists call this the principal-agent problem. What senior leaders really do is set the stage for an enterprise to do its job in the marketplace. In effect, CxOs create structures by which organizations generate their behavior. Going back to our chess analogy, this process would work as if our hypothetical CxO would say, "OK, let's let Joe handle the Knights and the Rooks. Sally will take care of the Bishops. I want Joe and Sally to huddle every move, especially in cases where their pieces are on the attack. Then I'll have Jim working the pawns…"—meta-chess, if you will.

Jay Forrester, the creator of the discipline of system dynamics once described the CEO as an "organization designer."[5] That is a much better way to describe the role than that of a chess player. Simple rules are the core of what it takes to make an organization work semiautonomously.

So what are those magic simple rules that will cause an organization to double its stock price? The answer lies in understanding the underlying "physics" of a given organization—different for every firm. Simulation models are an important tool in this regard. If one could abstract the organization into a model, one might test a wide range of simple rules, acted upon by "agents," to determine the implications of structure (sets of rules) on aggregate organizational performance. This style of modeling, which is already growing, is likely to gain in popularity in the coming years as senior leaders grapple with the ever-increasing complexity in organizations.

Redesigned Partnerships and Alliances

Business gets done when multiple organizations come together linked by a common goal. Sixteen major companies (and a host of smaller ones below that layer) form the ecosystem that builds the components for the iPhone.[6] It is hard to think of any core function of an organization that is done without suppliers, partners, technology providers, or coproducers. Yet for most organizations today, crafting the alliance is largely a legal procedure involving the exchange of documents. That leaves plenty of room for a more enlightened way to engineer a relationship among two or more firms through simulation.

I was once involved in the redesign of an industrial marine supply chain whose purpose was to deliver goods by boat from a supply base on shore to a series of offshore installations. On the one hand, there was the vessel supplier, in the business of chartering these vessels, with crews, to provide the transport of goods. On the other hand, there were the facility owners, the receivers of the goods. It was an astonishingly complex system, involving dozens of vessels—loading and unloading, whisking back and forth on a daily basis under an intricately timed delivery schedule. Unpredictable weather and equipment breakdowns conspired to ensure that no one day looked like any other.

All involved with this supply chain knew that it could be done more efficiently, resulting in fewer vessels needed to move the same amount of cargo. Yet the key to making it work was bringing the vessel charter operator into a jointly defined new supply chain configuration. But why would such a company work hard to *reduce* its revenue?

Keep in mind that this was an era and an environment in which large companies felt it was their sworn duty to beat their suppliers down for every penny they could (this is, unfortunately, still prevalent). When companies do this, suppliers will seek ways to lower their prices while maintaining acceptable margins by reducing any relationship-specific investments (technology or infrastructure that is bespoke to their customer that results in efficiencies), thereby creating a "hidden tax" that is passed back on to that customer. Counterintuitively, beating down the supplier on price results in a *higher* price than could be achieved through an intelligently designed partnership.

In our marine example, the two firms took the bold step of fashioning a gainsharing agreement between them: both firms would *equally share* any cost savings derived from reducing vessels from the fleet. That formed a positive invitation for our vessel company to participate in the development of a simulation model of the joint supply chain. Each firm's experts had a seat at the table as the model was built, and the result was dramatic. This supply chain performed far better, with fewer vessels, than any marine supply operation in the industry, and kicked off a wave of similar agreements extending to aviation and land transport.

In the future, partnerships will not simply be erected with paper documents, but rather will be engineered for value from the ground up, using simulation models that span buyer and supplier.

Talent on the Horizon

Much of my own unbridled optimism about the practice of problem solving in the future stems from my confidence in the class of talent that is on the verge of entering the professional domain. My interactions with legions of university undergraduate students and a few upper school students has shown me that this generation of folks has a very powerful attribute—they learn by doing, without fear. They assume they are two or three YouTube videos away from learning any subject, any time. While that may not be actually correct, the undaunted attitude toward learning is a potent enabler in the often headlong leap into complex problems.

That is the good news for hiring organizations. The challenge is that this generation will have higher fidelity choices when it comes to their formal education—"designer" degrees consisting of online stints across a variety of universities and corporate certifications will overtake the more traditional degrees. That is great for students, but it is much harder for the hiring organizations to assess new talent. Let me suggest that the assessments I outlined in chapter 7—"take home" exams—are a useful tool in this regard.

Ethical Dilemmas

It is inevitable that with the new powers of perception and prediction through problem solving, we will be drawn into the ethical consequences of their use. Consider these questions:

What if I invented a fancy wearable medical monitor that could predict the end of your (natural) life to within a few months?

What if I could predict the outcome of future elections so accurately that the losing side gets demoralized and doesn't show up at the polls on election day?

What if I could predict the likelihood of divorce for any newly engaged couple?

The capability to answer questions like these is near. The question is, *should* we answer them? I will concede that not every bit of analytics that can be done should be done. For this reason, ethical dilemmas should be taken out of the hands of problem solvers (who love to solve *any* problem), and instead put to ethicists to weigh in on the issues.

Chapter Summary

The future will be an exhilarating, terrifying place, filled with intricate problems to work on. The solutions that seem completely out of our grasp today will be feasible tomorrow, due to the confluence of tailwinds in technology, methodologies, and data. The skill of problem solving and the scientific thinking that underlies it will no longer be seen as a specialty— it will be assumed to be in each and every serious knowledge worker. The transformational power of science injected into business problems will spread to every corner of the economy, on every inch of the planet.

We must go beyond the problems of the day to seek evidence as to the size and shape of problems yet to come. That requires a constant scan of the horizon of promising methods and technologies, as I have outlined in this chapter.

It is a great time to be alive.

CHAPTER 9

Afterword

Let's have that personal conversation that I promised in the introduction to this book.

The conversation starts with a question: *where would you like to go from here?*

I challenge you to think very carefully and introspectively on this question so that you may formulate an answer that becomes the Rosetta Stone for your new life as a problem solver.

I've started two companies in the last dozen years of my career, and in both cases I set out to create the greatest problem-solving company the world had ever seen. That lofty goal led us to work on some awe-inspiring problems, some of which changed small corners of our global economy in rather significant ways. It has been fun. I loved it, all of it—the great times as well as the arduous climbs up from all of the disasters. It brought me tremendous joy to see our work in action, making a difference for worthy organizations and legions of people. Taking a retrospective view, it felt like our work *mattered*.

At this stage in my life, I am transitioning from a role of solving problems to a new role of sharing my ideas on problem solving with everyone willing to listen. Improving the lives of people grappling with highly complex problems is my chosen legacy. And I'm just getting started.

What is *your* circle of influence? Upon what class of problems (sometimes unseen) are you uniquely suited to act as a solver? Are you perhaps in a leadership role, ready to create teams of problem solvers and connect them to the organization's SMEs? Do you have an unusual blend of skills that map to a particular problem set? Do you learn new subjects much faster than others?

Perhaps you are as curious about societal problems as you are about business problems—poverty, disease, crime, malnutrition, addiction, injustice, war, terrorism, natural disasters. These kinds of problems are just as amenable to the problem-solving approaches grounded in science that we have covered in the preceding chapters. The largely untapped opportunity lies in applying a scientific approach to society's toughest problems.

No matter the problem, keep this in mind: "Tell a story."

This was the three-word advice given to me by a respected partner as our team was about to present a multiyear strategic plan to a major client. I barely even heard the words among the noises in my head clamoring for attention. In the end, we did well, although I can't even remember what I said to the client. But those three words came back to me when it was all over.

"Tell a story."

Some of the best advice is the simplest. What I believe he was saying in a compact way was to focus on the message, punctuate that message with artifacts and exhibits, set context, draw clear conclusions. We are not here merely to exchange information—we are here to advocate for a cause we believe in. And we will *prove* it systematically, objectively, and methodically with our models and data.

The phrase eventually became my mantra for everything we did at my companies. It is a deliberate, thoughtful action that suggests that anything you say, any exhibit you show must all fit into the larger scheme of your analysis. As with all good stories, you need a beginning, a plot, a climax, and an end. Sequence is vital. Words mean things. Clean design is paramount. Style matters.

By now you know that problem solving is not just about numbers. Skillful analysis is about telling the whole truth in an engaging, even inspiring way. Great companies recognize this and encourage it in all of the important activities they do. The very best organizations *institutionalize* the behavior with company norms, available tools, and ubiquitous messaging.

My goal here was to turn you into an amazing storyteller—an advocate for intelligent change armed with cogent facts and data and calculations.

Do your job well and you will be the stuff of great leadership at work and in life, no matter your title.

Whatever angle you take on solving problems using science, the passion with which you pursue problems will be the force that propels you forward. This book was not intended to be a detached recipe for implementing the latest faddish incremental change in organizational performance, but rather a manifesto for radically rethinking everything the organization does in a way that creates long-term valuable systems that act to our benefit. Dramatic action requires passionate actors. You must love what you do, to do it well for the long run. And it should feel more like fun than work.

Failure will be the ever-present dragon at the gates, coming at a far higher rate than most organizations are used to seeing. Failure is a signature feature of the experimentalist culture that surrounds good problem solving. While you do not set out to fail, being circumspect about it and learning from it should be standard operating procedure. Conversely, celebrate unmistakably successful solutions with gusto—noble work deserves it.

Corporate gravity tends to distill everything into a rigid, mechanized set of guidelines and procedures, process specifications, and standards. That leaves very little room for serendipity and learning, two vital aspects of problem solving. Imagine asking a police detective when a crime is scheduled to be solved. There is no schedule, but instead there is a process of looking at evidence and acting on those findings. Problem solving is not immune to proper project management procedure, but can be killed by overzealous application of bureaucratic processes that are more suitable to uniform and predictable tasks. Don't let the forces of gravity slowly defeat good problem solving. A champion for the cause is crucial. If you have made it this far in the book, that champion is probably you.

There are wise, experienced people in every organization, many of whom do not label themselves as problem-solving experts, but do embody all of the qualities that we have discussed here. Seek out those individuals as mentors—for exceptional problem solving requires many voices blended together. Then, endeavor to become a mentor, step by step, problem by problem. Legacies are created over the entirety of your career, not just at the latter stages. Start that process now. Become the enabling force that ushers in a new era of performance for the organization.

The undeniable truth is that the reward for winning the game in life, as it is in pinball, is the chance to play again.

There are problems out there waiting to be solved.

It's your turn.

Notes

2 Methods and Madness

1. Wolfram Research Inc., *Mathematica*, Version 10.0 Champaign, IL (2014).

3 Data

1. Parts of this example were extracted from the Fake Names Generator at http://names.igopaygo.com/.

4 The Art of Science: Visualization

1. Ray Kurzweil, *How to Create a Mind* (London: Viking Adult, 2012).
2. "Lean Thinking," Wikipedia, accessed April 2015. http://en.wikipedia.org/wiki/Lean_Thinking.
3. Generally speaking, I am not a fan of rigid standards that stifle creativity, but in this case I make an exception. Enforcing ICOM gives your diagrams a consistently clean, readable quality.
4. Knowledge Based Systems, Inc. http://www.idef.com/idef0.htm.
5. "Sankey Diagram," Wikipedia, accessed March 2015. http://en.wikipedia.org/wiki/Sankey_diagram.
6. "Treemapping," Wikipedia, accessed April 2015. http://en.wikipedia.org/wiki/Treemapping.

5 Tools of the Trade: The Technology of Problem Solving

1. Formally, this is often referred to as an entity relationship diagram (ERD), but one need not adhere to each and every syntax rule of ERDs in order to generate a useful representation of the data structure one is creating to feed the model.
2. Please refer to ProfitFromScience's website at http://www.business-laboratory.com/profitfromscience, where I will periodically review and comment on software applications for problem solving.

3. Google, Inc. https://code.google.com/p/kml-samples/.

6 Using Your New Superpower

1. If your code does not work this way or you find it very difficult to do forensics on your code, this is usually a signal that the code is not structured correctly. Consider revising your approach to the code to make it more amenable to forensics

7 Setting the Stage: The Making of a Great Problem-Solving Team

1. Michael Lewis, *Moneyball* (New York: W. W. Norton & Company, 2004).
2. The term "smart creative" was coined in Eric Schmidt, Jonathan Rosenberg, *How Google Works* (New York: Grand Central Publishing, 2014).
3. This is a heavily stylized example from a real case from our practice.
4. Clayton M. Christensen, Richard Alton, Curtis Rising, and Andrew Waldeck, "The Big Idea: The New M&A Playbook," *Harvard Business Review*, March 2011.
5. This is sometimes referred to as "sweeping the solution space," wind-tunneling, or even stress testing.

8 Implications for the Future

1. "Driverless Car," Wikipedia, accessed April 2015. http://en.wikipedia.org/wiki/Google_driverless_car.
2. Sensors and housings are not included in that price.
3. Stephen Wolfram, Stephen Wolfram, LLC, *A .data Top-Level Domain?* http://blog.stephenwolfram.com/2012/01/a-data-top-level-internet-domain/.
4. "Richard Santulli," Wikipedia, accessed May 2015. http://en.wikipedia.org/wiki/Richard_Santulli.
5. Mark Keough and Andrew Doman, "The CEO as Organization Designer," *The McKinsey Quarterly*, No. 2, Spring 1992.
6. http://www.businessinsider.com/meet-the-companies-that-make-the-iphone-2012-5#.

Index